Come, sinners, to the gospel feast;

Let every soul be Jesu's guest;

Ye need not one be left behind,

For God hath bidden all mankind.

Charles Wesley

ATONE

The Difference the Cross Makes

WIL CANTRELL

AT**ONE**
The Difference the Cross Makes
©2021 Wil Cantrell

books@marketsquarebooks.com
P.O. Box 23664   Knoxville, Tennessee 37933
ISBN: 978-1-950899-17-3
Library of Congress: 2020951623

Printed and Bound in the United States of America
Cover Illustration & Book Design ©2021 Market Square Publishing, LLC
Publisher: Kevin Slimp
Editor: Kristin Lighter
Post-Process Editor: Ken Rochelle

All rights reserved. No part of this book may be reproduced in any manner without written permission except in the case of brief quotations included in critical articles and reviews. For information, please contact Market Square Publishing, LLC.

Unless noted otherwise, Scripture quotations are from:

New Revised Standard Version Bible
copyright © 1989 National Council of the Churches of Christ
in the United States of America.
Used by permission. All rights reserved worldwide.

Table of Contents

Introduction

On a Hill Far Away 1

Chapter One:

Why Did Jesus Have to Die? 7

Chapter Two:

Forgiveness and Everything that Comes With It 25

Chapter Three:

The Great War 49

Chapter Four:

A New Nature. 71

Chapter Five:

The Family You Never Knew You Had 91

Chapter Six:

For All 113

Epilogue. 127

INTRODUCTION
On a Hill Far Away

On a spring day sometime around 30 AD, a group of Roman soldiers hastily crucified three Jewish criminals on a hill outside Jerusalem. Crucifixion was a torturous affair which usually took days to claim the life of its victim. This time, however, it was shortened to several hours so the execution would not interfere with the upcoming Passover festival.

Everything went according to plan. They beat one of the criminals so badly before crucifying him that he expired just a few hours after being nailed to the cross. Shortly thereafter, they broke the legs of the other criminals so they could no longer push themselves up to breathe, hastening their death by suffocation.

Several notable events occurred that day. From noon till 3pm, massive storm clouds moved in making the sky almost as dark as night. Some people reported feeling earthquake tremors in and around Jerusalem.

One of the criminals, a controversial religious teacher, kept talking about forgiving those who were crucifying and humiliating him. Unusual behavior, for sure. And reports from the Jerusalem temple indicate in the middle of the afternoon a massive curtain in the temple inexplicably ripped in two from top to bottom.

While these events produced no small amount of conversation, they seem to have made no immediate lasting impact on the residents and festival goers in the city. By sundown the bodies had been disposed of, and life went on like it always had.

No one seemed to think much more about that day until a few months later as travelers once again streamed into the city for another festival, this one known as Pentecost. At that time, several former friends of the executed religious leader began to proclaim that his death had fundamentally changed the course of human history and humanity's relationship with God.

As you might guess, most people who heard their message rejected it. Some even accused them of being drunk. Still, they kept at it, sharing their message in every language spoken within the city. Surprisingly, their persistence paid off. By the end of the day, three thousand people committed their lives to following the ways of the crucified preacher, Jesus of Nazareth, whom they soon began to call Jesus Christ.

For the next three centuries, more and more people throughout the Mediterranean world came to believe Jesus' death foundationally altered the human condition and began following his teachings. Eventually, even the Roman Empire – which oversaw Jesus' crucifixion – took Christianity as its official religion, ensuring the story of Jesus' death would spread throughout Asia, Africa, and Europe. Today, almost one third of the world's population believes what happened that day on that cross changed the course of history and eternity.

According to the story Jesus' followers tell, his death on the cross provided a way for humanity to be **at one** with God. Christians describe the end of their estrangement from their Creator made possible by Jesus' sacrificial death as **atonement**, which you might find helpful to think of as at-one-ment. Interestingly, while the Christian Church in all its diverse forms throughout the centuries has always based its foundational teachings around the work of atonement accomplished through Jesus' crucifixion, Christians have never agreed on exactly **HOW** Jesus' death set them at one with God.

In the earliest days of the Christian movement, followers simply described the difference Jesus' death on the cross made in their own words. Over the centuries, these descriptions were expanded and codified by theologians who produced what became known as theories of atonement. Written with great detail as if to stand up in a court of law or a scientific journal, each of these theories describes an aspect of the difference Jesus' death makes. Today, many Christian theologians identify seven main theories of atonement, though it is possible to identify as many as fifteen or more distinct theories of atonement in Christian history.

Thank God we do not have to understand every detail of every theory for our lives to be transformed by Jesus' death on the cross for us. If there is one thing that binds together all these theories, which can vary greatly in their explanations of Jesus' death, it is that in each explanation, Jesus dies for us.

Perhaps you already know the life changing power of Jesus' death and you are reading this book to draw closer to the One who gave his life for you. If so, it is my prayer that these pages will fill you with a new appreciation for the depth of Jesus' love which can only be found through a deep dive into the nature of his sacrifice.

Or perhaps you are amazed by Jesus' ongoing influence, but unsure about the truth of the claims made about him. You may even be wondering how any of the claims his followers make about him can be true when so many of the claims vary so greatly. Rest assured, you are not the first nor will you be the last to ask these questions. In fact, you are asking questions which I believe God intentionally created every human heart to contemplate. My prayer for you is that this book will help you consider your questions within the context of what we know about Jesus' life, and the difference Jesus has made in the lives of billions of people over thousands of years.

Ultimately, I believe we will find it impossible to describe all that was accomplished through Jesus' death in one or two or even fifteen neat and tidy theoretical descriptions. Exactly **HOW** Jesus changed the world through his sacrifice may be so great a mystery that human words will never be able to do it justice. When we come up against the limits of our language to describe the work of God, we do well to remember the wisest within the Christian movement have always cautioned us to be prepared for moments when our words will fail us in our attempts to describe a Creator who is greater than the minds of his creatures can comprehend.

I do believe, however, that it is possible to understand and to experience **WHAT** it is that Jesus' death makes possible for us. And it is to that task, of both seeking to understand and to experience the life changing power of Jesus' death, that we now turn as we begin chapter one with a question first asked on that day long ago by those at the foot of Jesus' cross: Why did Jesus have to die?

CHAPTER ONE
Why Did Jesus Have to Die?

"Why did Jesus have to die? I mean, if God's powerful enough to do anything, couldn't God have saved us another way?"

I'd heard a variation of this question many times in late night conversations with friends in our college dorm rooms, in my own head as a young adult wrestling with my faith, and even in conversations with men and women who have been studying the scriptures and following Christ for much longer than I have been alive. This time, however, the question came from a twelve-year-old girl during Sunday school class.

As the pastor, I had stopped by the 6th grade class that Sunday to show my support for the teachers and to crack a few jokes with the kids. So when the question came up, I just grinned and waited to see how the teachers would answer. "This should be fun. Let's see how they handle this one," I thought to myself. My smile wore off as I realized the teachers had no intention of answering the question. They, along with all the students, were staring directly at me.

Taken at face value, it's the most basic and most impossible question that can be asked about the Christian faith. A faith system centered around a crucified Savior should at minimum be able to articulate exactly why the Savior had to die. At the same time, to say that Jesus had to die could be taken as a denial of God's power. As the young lady astutely pointed out with her question, wasn't God powerful enough to save us another way? On the other hand, to say that Jesus didn't have to die would be to accuse God of requiring Jesus to endure unnecessary suffering, an idea critics of Christianity have often termed divine child abuse.

Answering that Jesus had to die meant implying God was impotent to save us any other way. Answering that Jesus did not have to die made God into a cruel monster. And not answering the question directly was akin to admitting there was no rational basis at all for the Christian religion.

I decided to start my response by acknowledging that God can do anything except one thing. God cannot be untrue to God's own nature. While we humans often act in ways that are contrary to our beliefs and values, God never does. God is the only completely authentic being in the universe.

Yes, God could choose simply to cancel the consequences of our sins and allow us all into heaven with nothing more than a snap of the fingers. But since God instead chose such a costly way of saving us, there must be a good reason why, and the reason why must be found in the very nature of God.

The Bible teaches us that God is love.[1] And in calling upon God as "Father," Jesus teaches us the closest human analogy for the love of God is the love of a parent for a child. So, if God is love and we are God's children, then by God's nature God must always do what is best for God's children.

When a parent and child become estranged, overcoming the estrangement is costly. I've never seen a family reunite without terribly difficult deliberations. While many families learn to simply tolerate each other again after a season of estrangement, a family that truly wants to be a family again must do much more substantial gut-wrenching work.

When it comes to overcoming our estrangement from God brought about by our sinful ways of living for our selfish desires rather than by God's design, reconciliation is neither cheap nor easy. In the Old Testament

---

[1] 1 John 4:8

book of Jeremiah, God condemns unfaithful priests and prophets saying, "They have healed the wound of my people lightly, saying, 'Peace, peace,' when there is no peace."[2]

The prophets and priests were telling the people everything was okay when everything was not okay. They were allowing the people to continue living out of greed and self-interest while using religious rituals to massage their egos and assuage their guilt. God wants to bring about real forgiveness, real healing, and real restoration - not just lip service.

In the 20th century, the great German theologian and anti-Nazi dissident, Dietrich Bonhoeffer, cautioned us to be wary of cheap grace which offers "forgiveness without repentance", "grace without discipleship", and "grace without the cross". Instead, Bonhoeffer directs us to pursue costly grace: grace that "costs a man his life" and "cost God the life of His Son."[3] Bonhoeffer had seen how the Christian religion corrupted by cheap grace was used to numb the people of Germany from their guilt, thereby allowing them to commit genocide while still believing they were good, honest, faithful people. He knew the only grace that could really save was costly grace.

---

[2] Jeremiah 6:14, English Standard Version.

[3] Dietrich Bonhoeffer, The Cost of Discipleship (Simon & Schuster, 1995), 44-45.

God refused to heal the estrangement brought about by sin lightly or cheaply. God paid the highest price. A price so high that even Jesus himself asked his Father if there was another way it could be accomplished when he prayed just before his arrest, "My Father, if it is possible, let this cup pass from me; yet not what I want but what you want."[4] The answer Jesus received to his prayer and the truth the world has struggled with ever since is that there wasn't another way because nothing else could accomplish what Jesus' death could.

Why did Jesus have to die? Jesus had to die because it was the only way to put us, the real us, at one with God, the real God.

Jesus did not die to save the people we pretend to be, the people who numb ourselves to the work of evil in our lives by convincing our egos we are good, honest, hard-working people who deserve forgiveness and salvation. Jesus died to save people like you and me who have an incredible capacity for evil and self-deception.

Nor did Jesus die to put us at one with a pretend God, who wants everyone merely to get along and subscribe to a few basic theological beliefs. Jesus died to put us at one with the real, living, wild God: The God described in the Old Testament as a jealous lover who will pay any price to win His beloved back, and in the New Testament

---

[4] Matthew 26:39

as the Father who would allow his prodigal son to walk away from the family in hopes he might one day return as someone capable of being a real part of the family. This is why Jesus had to die.

When I finished speaking, I noticed the Sunday school teachers were smiling. I'd like to think they were smiling because they liked what I had to say so much, though it may well have been because I took up most of the class time with my answer, which made their teaching responsibilities that day much more manageable. The young lady who asked the question was sitting up tall in her chair and looking directly at me, aware that she had posed a question of great importance. Several of the boys in the class were snickering in the back, most likely more to convince each other that their inside jokes were funny, rather than because they actually were funny.

I'm not sure how much the students and teachers remember about that class. I certainly don't expect they would remember all the details of my answer. I do hope some of them found themselves invited into a conversation which began with Jesus himself and which will continue until Jesus returns. And it is into that same conversation which I would now like to invite you.

In preparation for writing this book, I have been spending my devotional time reading the entire crucifixion narratives from the four Gospels each morning. I am convinced the Biblical witness directs us to three reasons Jesus died on the cross, which encapsulate all the various atonement theories.

- Jesus died to offer us forgiveness and salvation.
- Jesus died to defeat the powers of evil.
- Jesus died to make us like Him by transforming us back into the image of God in which we were created.

Forgiveness and the Assurance of Salvation

When a relationship becomes estranged, forgiveness must always precede reconciliation. In most cases, each person has done something wrong. Though often, one party is the much more serious offender. Generally, reconciliation occurs when the person who is most in the wrong finds a way to express their sorrow for their actions and their renewed commitment to the relationship by making amends. In response, the person who was hurt begins to let go of their anger towards the other person (forgiveness), and in some cases also begins to allow the relationship to become intimate again (reconciliation). This is the common usage of the word, atone: to make amends for past wrongs in the hope of bringing about reconciliation.

The atonement we see take place through the cross is very different. In an early conversation about the meaning of the cross, Paul told the Christians in Corinth, "...in Christ God was reconciling the world to himself, not counting their trespasses against them, and entrusting the message of reconciliation to us."[5] Here Paul is drawing upon a Roman legal term, reconciliation, to describe the work of Christ. In the legal world of Paul's day, reconciliation was the process by which the party in the wrong, or the party which lost the battle and is thereby assumed to be in the wrong since the winners usually write the history, makes amends by offering extravagant gifts to the other party, thereby bringing about peace and re-establishing a basis for the relationship.

Paul, alone among ancient writers, uses the term reconciliation in a very different manner. For Paul, God's way of atoning for the sins of the people and bringing about reconciliation requires God, the party in the right, to give an extravagant gift – the life of His own Son – to the us, the party in the wrong. Nowhere else can we find an example in the ancient Roman world of the word reconciliation being used to describe the restoration of a relationship brought about by the party in the right paying the price.

Our estrangement from God brought about by sin is so great we could not offer adequate amends to reestablish

---

[5] 2 Corinthians 5:19

the relationship even if we tried. So the wild, living God, the Father desperately in love with His children, does so on our behalf. Through Jesus' death we discover the price has been paid for our sins to be forgiven and for us to be reconciled into close relationship with God, for now and for eternity. While on the cross, Jesus acknowledges his intention to forgive and save by praying for the soldiers who were crucifying him, "Father, forgive them, for they do not know what they are doing"[6] and by assuring the thief on the cross beside him, "Today, you will be with me in paradise."[7]

Acknowledging our need of such costly forgiveness is no small task. A few years ago, while working with a recovery ministry, I became familiar with the 12 Steps, first articulated by Alcoholics Anonymous. I could not believe how much the 12 Steps seemed to succinctly sum up the core of Jesus' teachings. Specifically, I marveled at the wisdom of steps one and two.

- Step 1 – We admitted we were powerless over our addictions and compulsive behaviors – that our lives had become unmanageable.
- Step 2 – Came to believe that a Power greater than ourselves could restore us to sanity.

---

[6] Luke 23:34

[7] Luke 23:43

The path to healing and wholeness for the addict begins with the unapologetic acknowledgment they cannot save themselves. Their only hope is a power greater than themselves. It is the same for the Christian.

Our only hope is that Christ paid a price high enough to forgive us for the way we have intentionally and unintentionally harmed others, the ways we have ignored God's presence and turned a deaf ear to God's call upon our lives, and the ways we have perverted God's good gifts of power, sex, money, and pleasure in failed attempts to find fulfillment outside of God's design for our lives.

Accepting the forgiveness and salvation Christ alone can offer frees us from lives of guilt, shame, self-loathing, and self-medicating. Though we cannot earn the gift, it comes with a high price: our very lives. Those who have taken Jesus at his word, that they could find life by giving up their lives and taking up their crosses to follow Him,[8] will tell you it is the best thing they have ever done.

For some of them, the power of their experience is such, they do not spend much time worrying about the details of how Jesus saved them, because they are so enthralled by the fact that Jesus saved them. For others, these stories seem too good to be true. "Is Jesus

---

[8] Matthew 16:24-25

actually a Savior?" they ask. "Or is believing Jesus to be a Savior just a convenient, religious way to numb ourselves from our struggle with guilt, shame, and meaninglessness?"

To answer the question of whether Jesus is actually a Savior, Christian leaders quickly began positing theories of atonement. The most prominent are the Ransom theory, Christ died to buy humanity back from enslavement to the devil; the Satisfaction theory, Jesus died to satisfy God's wrath stirred up by the sins of humanity and God's demand for justice to be carried out; and the Substitution theory, Jesus substituted himself to be the recipient of the suffering humanity deserves so humanity could experience right relationship with God which only Jesus deserves.

In Chapter 3, we will turn our attention to exploring these theories of how Jesus' death offers us forgiveness and salvation in more detail, and how we can experience for ourselves the truth behind these theories. For now, let's turn our attention from the difference the cross makes for us personally to the difference the cross makes cosmically.

Victory in Jesus

Jesus' public life began with forty days in the wilderness where he was tempted by the devil. It ended with darkness covering the land from noon till 3pm as he hung on the cross. At 3pm, he cried out in a loud voice, "It is finished."[9] As he died, an earthquake shook the ground and the curtain in the temple was inexplicably torn in two.[10] It was as if a battle much larger than any eye could see was being waged.

Could it be that the darkness that afternoon symbolized the powers of darkness Jesus was confronting on the cross? Could the earthquake be emblematic of the changing nature of the world following Jesus' death? And was the ripping of the massive curtain in the Temple, which serving as a barrier separating the Holy of Holies where the Ark of the Covenant was kept from the rest of the Temple, meant to tell us every power that could keep humanity from encountering God had now been defeated?

Early Christians certainly seem to believe this to be the case. When Jesus was arrested, he himself told his captors "...this is your hour and the power of darkness!"[11] indicating he saw their actions as part of a cosmic battle between good and evil. A few years later, Paul advised the church at Ephesus to "Put on the whole armor of God, so that you may be able to stand against

---

[9] John 19:30

[10] Matthew 27:51

[11] Luke 22:53

the wiles of the devil. For our struggle is not against enemies of blood and flesh, but against the rulers, against the authorities, against the cosmic powers of this present darkness, against the spiritual forces of evil in the heavenly places."[12] Apparently, Paul understood Christian life to be part of a cosmic war which Jesus had won, but in which battles still raged.

So, it shouldn't surprise us that Christians would want to understand how Jesus won this war against evil on the cross, and why it is that battles with evil still go on even after the Jesus' crucifixion and resurrection.

You may struggle to believe in the concept of the devil. I'll admit the idea of a devil who is God's equal and opposite is absurd. God has no equals. God is the creator of all. God is the only eternal being. If there is a devil, then the devil must be a creature. A creature, by definition, can never be as powerful as the creator.

Before you give up entirely on the idea of a devil, however, and conclude as many have that the devil we read about in the Bible is just a literary device the writers' used to personify evil, let me ask you this: Do you really think Jesus went out to the wilderness to do battle with a personification or with something real? Yes, the idea of a devil who is equal to God and eternal like God is ridiculous. But the idea of a fallen angel who

---

[12] Ephesians 6:11-12

used free will to turn against God might not be so crazy since we know God certainly provides humanity with that same free will and ability to oppose their creator.

Now, even if this whole talk of a devil at all is just too much for you to take, ask yourself this question: Do you think the power of evil is at work in our world? And for God's kingdom to come and God's will to be done on earth as it is in heaven, do you think the power of evil is going to need to be defeated? A brief glance at history and the current state of our society seem to provide more than enough evidence to the affirmative.

Evil and its offspring, self-interest, are woven into the fabric of our lives and our world. While it is tempting to think of history as constantly moving incrementally in a positive direction, the actual evidence is more ambiguous. For those of us living in the United States, we are only a little over 150 years removed from the abolition of one of the cruelest forms of slavery ever known, with atrocities far surpassing the sufferings inflicted upon the Hebrew slaves by the Egyptians prior to the Exodus and greater in its cruelty than the types of slavery practiced in the Mediterranean world during Jesus' time.

Today, we live in a society where it has never been more politically incorrect to call into question the equality of any person or group of people, yet we simultaneously live in a society in which our laws and policies have led to over forty years of increasingly unequal access and opportunity among people of different classes and colors. In a world like this, how are we to believe that good will ultimately triumph over evil and right over might?

Christians find this answer in the cross. On the cross, Jesus confronts evil at its worst and defeats it. Though the powers of evil crucify him, Jesus' resurrection proves his triumph over evil and his power over death. According to this line of thinking about atonement which eventually came to be called the Christus Victor theory of Atonement, God does not pay off the devil as the Ransom theory stresses. God defeats the devil thus allowing humanity the freedom to live in the confidence that the only power evil has over us is the power we voluntarily give it.

In Chapter 3, we will consider the difference knowing evil has already been defeated makes in our personal battles with evil and the destructive self-interest it spawns.

Restoring the Image

In work of Jesus on the cross to forgive sins, grant salvation, and defeat evil we see God overcoming the power of sin and death. Yet even these great victories do not encompass the entirety of Jesus' work on our behalf through his death. Jesus did not die just so we could go to heaven. Jesus died so that we could be fit for heaven when we get there. To put it another way, the goal of Christianity is not just for everyone to like Christ, it is for everyone to become like Christ. If you have not become like Christ, you won't enjoy heaven very much, even if you make it there.

Jesus was very clear in his teachings that he desired for people to imitate him, and in so doing, to have the image of God in which they were created restored in their lives. He told them the greatest form of love was to lay down your life for your friends[13] and then invited them to take up their crosses and follow him as he went about befriending people they considered their enemies.[14]

In 1 Corinthians 11:1, the Apostle Paul describes the Christian life like this:

Be imitators of me as I am of Christ.

Paul's entire approach to Christianity could be summed up as *Be like Christ and then invite others to be like you.*

On the cross, Jesus showed humanity the greatest depth of love as he died for his friends and his enemies.

---

[13] John 15:13

[14] Matthew 16:24

Through imitating this love, humanity is transformed into the image of Christ and participates in making human society more like the kingdom of God.

First articulated prominently by Augustine of Hippo in the latter 300s and early 400s, these ideas came to be known as the *moral influence theory of atonement* after being picked up by French philosopher, Peter Abelard, in the 12th Century.

In Chapter 4, we will take a deeper look at the moral influence theory and how Jesus' death on the cross fundamentally changes our vision of morality and human potential.

The Fullness of God

Even in these preliminary discussions of the various ways of understanding the difference the cross makes, I imagine you are mostly likely already finding yourself resonating with some ways more than others. However, I would ask you to keep your mind open to all three major ways of understanding the difference the cross makes.

While one of the ways may be truer to your personal experience of life thus far, the reason the church has never selected one way as the true way to understand the cross and rejected the others is because it is only by embracing the forgiveness, salvation, victory over evil, and moral transformation made possible by Jesus' death that we can experience the fullness of what it means to be at one with God.

CHAPTER TWO

Forgiveness and Everything that Comes With It

When I was 10 years old, I began to hear a lot of talk about getting saved at church. Prior to this age, the main emphases I picked up on at church had more to do with loving God, loving your neighbor, and learning the Bible stories. Now, I became aware that many of the church leaders felt I needed to get saved. Otherwise, I would be incapable of loving God and my neighbor and, even worse, if I didn't get saved, I might end up in hell for eternity.

The idea of hell scared the hell out of my younger self. The looming challenges of middle school and puberty seemed scary enough. I didn't want to have to worry about hell also. So, I began to ask how someone like me could be saved. The response I got was straight forward enough and basically only required three steps:

1) Believe Jesus died for your sins.

2) Ask Jesus to forgive your sins.

3) Commit your life to serving Christ.

If you did these three things, I was told, you would begin to feel the Holy Spirit living inside of you and you would experience the joy of knowing you would be spending eternity in heaven with Jesus.

It sounded like a pretty good deal to me. Pray a simple prayer. Avoid eternal punishment. Acquire peace and joy. Got it.

Naturally, I chose to pray to be saved by asking Jesus to forgive my sins, most of which at that time in my life had been committed directly against my sister, and I told Jesus I would do whatever he wanted me to do with my life, though I hedged my commitment slightly by admitting I really didn't want to be a missionary in Africa because after listening to an African missionary speak at our church, it sounded to me like the food in Africa probably didn't taste very good, and beyond that they had lions roaming around over there and who knows what else.

After praying this prayer, I waited for peace, joy, and assurance to flood over me. They never did. So, I kept praying the prayer, convinced that I must not be praying it sincerely enough. Otherwise, surely, I would experience the feelings I had been told to expect. Still nothing. Finally, as I was praying the prayer for the umpteenth time, this time while on a church mission trip, I heard God speak. Rather than assuring me I was saved and giving me all the peace and joy I had been hoping for, God simply said this: "Wait."

"Seriously, God, that's all you've got to say to me?" I thought to myself. Still, I decided to give waiting a try and trust that God would give me the experiences I needed when the time was right. I occasionally worried a little about not receiving any assurance of salvation, especially when well-meaning friends asked me if I knew where I'd be going if I died that night in a car accident. But I figured if I died while waiting as God instructed me and God sent me to hell, then that would make God the biggest punk around. Since no one close to me seemed to think God was a punk, I felt fairly secure in my spiritual status and put the whole getting saved thing onto the back-burner of my mind.

For the next seven years, I continued my research into the topics of sin – mainly through daily living, and salvation – mainly by attending church. As you might guess, my research on sin was much more extensive than my contemplations about salvation. Thankfully for my sister and unfortunately for everyone else, I greatly diversified my sin portfolio during these years. Lying to avoid embarrassment, cheating on schoolwork, lust, underage drinking, as well as standing by and doing nothing while an innocent student was bullied for fear of the bully turning his wrath in my direction became experiences with which I was intimately familiar.

Luckily, during this stormy season of life, I was invited to go on another church trip. Once again there was a lot of talk on the retreat about the importance of accepting God's forgiveness. Rather than focusing on seeking forgiveness primarily to avoid hell, this time the focus was on how Jesus looks at us with love even when we are stuck in the filthy depths of our sin. For the first time, I came to see that Jesus died for me at my very worst, not at my best, and that he looked down at me from his cross with eyes of compassion, not condemnation.

Each word spoken that weekend about Jesus' love for sinners chipped away at the walls I had erected to protect my insecure heart. Until at last, the walls came crashing down. Tears flooded my eyes and I didn't even care that I was crying in front of other teenage boys, a predicament I previously would have thought of as closely akin to hell. Time and again I marveled at the thought, "He loves me so much. How can he possibly love me so much?"

Once more, I found myself praying a prayer quite similar to the one I had prayed seven years previously. "Jesus, I believe you died for me. Jesus, forgive me of my sins. Jesus, I give my whole life, every bit of it to you." The wait was over. Peace and joy engulfed my heart.

And at the deepest level of my being, I knew that I knew this Jesus, who loved me, would not let go of me, now or ever, for all eternity.

Years later, I read the words written by my spiritual ancestor John Wesley in his journal on May 24, 1738 and knew exactly what he meant when he described his own spiritual awakening by saying, "I felt I did trust in Christ, Christ alone for salvation, and an assurance was given me that he had taken away my sins, even mine, and saved me from the law of sin and death."

I wonder if that's why on the day of Pentecost long ago, three thousand people responded to the stubborn preaching of former fishermen by committing their lives to the crucified rabbi from Nazareth. As the words of disciples filled their ears, did a vision come to their eyes of Jesus, the one whose death they had demanded, looking down from the cross with love and forgiveness? At their core, did they come to realize that they were cherished by God more deeply than they ever dared to dream?

I believe they did. I believe it was their experiences and thousands upon thousands more similar experiences in the years that followed which caused early Christians to begin to try to articulate logically the truth they discovered experientially - that Jesus could forgive their sins and grant them eternal life.

Forgiving Sins & Opening the Gates of Heaven

Throughout his ministry, Jesus had a controversial habit of forgiving sins. In fact, his habit of forgiving sins infuriated the scribes and Pharisees so much they began to plot to have him killed.

In one instance, when asked to heal a paralyzed man, Jesus responds by telling the man his sins are forgiven. The Jewish religious leaders immediately became enraged at Jesus for presuming to forgive sins, since in Jewish theology only God could forgive sins. In response to their anger, Jesus tells the man to get up and walk.[15]

On another occasion, a sinful woman seeks Jesus out while he is eating at the house of Simon the Pharisee. While the rest of dinner party felt Jesus should not dignify her with his attention, Jesus reassures the woman that her sins are forgiven and that she has been saved.[16] As you can imagine, Simon and his Pharisee friends were not happy with Jesus at all.

In the last moments of his life on the cross, Jesus continued to offer forgiveness and salvation to those nearby. As he looked upon the soldiers who were crucifying him, he prays "Father, forgive them; for they do

---

[15] Matthew 9:2-8, Mark 2:1-2, & Luke 5:17-26

[16] Luke 7:36-50

not know what they are doing."[17] And in response to the penitent criminal crucified beside him, Jesus promises the man, "Today you will be with me in paradise."[18]

The religious leaders of Jesus' day were correct to be shocked anyone would dare to forgive sins and offer eternal salvation. Only God can forgive sins because sin by definition is a transgression against God and only God can extend eternal salvation because only God is eternal. The mistake the religious leaders made was not recognizing Jesus' special relationship with God the Father.

Sin and Salvation Today

In past generations, people worried a great deal about finding forgiveness and salvation. This isn't necessarily the case today. A recent survey by Lifeway Research found persons between the ages of 18-44 are more than twice as likely to believe that sin does not exist as compared to persons 45 and older.[19] As more and more people question the concepts of sin and the need for salvation, they are increasing likely to see their failures as something other than sin. Instead, they see often see their failures as mental health issues and attribute

---

[17] Luke 23:34

[18] Luke 23:43

[19] LifeWay Research. American Views on Sin, 2016. http://lifewayresearch.com/wp-content/uploads/2017/08/Sept-2016-American-Views-on-Sin.pdf

many of them to societal forces beyond their control as well as their own personality quirks. Naturally, they look for healing through counseling and self-help resources, more so than religion and repentance. From this perspective, they worry very little about hell and instead assume, if there is life after death, they will go to a good place when they die so long as they try their best to be a decently good person.

No one should deny the reality of mental health struggles nor the clear evidence that many times counseling along with medication are the best pathways back to health. There are certainly circumstances which in previous ages we might have identified as sin, today we would rightly see more as mental health challenges. In the past, a child who performs poorly in school and lashes out at their parents would have been labeled a moral failure for their sinful laziness and defiance. Today, we've learned to ask whether Attention Deficit Hyperactivity Disorder might be preventing this child from being able to concentrate on schoolwork and if their defiance at home might be coming from the frustration caused by their inability to keep up with their classmates academically despite their best efforts.

Even so, the reality of mental health issues should not blind us to the reality of sin. There are instances when mental health issues lead to sin and vice-versa.

Consider the case of the young man who struggles to make a commitment to his significant other. They care deeply for one another, and they each have stable jobs which will allow their marriage to begin with a solid financial foundation. Everyone knows she is ready to get married and start a family. Still, he just won't buy the ring and pop the question.

It would be easy to label the young man an immature playboy so consumed by selfishness that he can't commit his life to one woman. On the other hand, it's possible his problems have less to do with selfishness and more to do with his fear of abandonment. Perhaps he lost a parent at an early age, maybe his parents struggled with addiction and were never there for him when he needed them, or possibly he saw his parents go through an ugly divorce. He may not be worried about his ability to commit to her. He might be worried about whether she'll always be there for him since the only other people he ever trusted to support him always let him down.

In his case, it's not his fault he is struggling with commitment. What he does about it, however, is his responsibility. If he does not eventually commit to her, then he is sinning by being an unfaithful steward of the love God gave them for each other, inflicting deep seated emotional pain into her life, and wasting her time by stringing her along in a relationship which was never going to go anywhere. Ultimately, the question becomes will he courageously seek out the help he needs to overcome his fear of commitment, or will his sinful cowardice allow his fear to continue controlling his life. If he does not find it within himself to confront his fear, he will leave a wake of other chaos and brokenness which will only deepen his mental health struggles and increase his alienation from God.

What is Sin?

For those who still believe in sin, sin is usually thought of as doing bad things God does not want you to do. This definition isn't wrong. It's just incomplete.

From a Biblical perspective, sin is both an orientation and a distance. Consider the story of Adam and Eve in Genesis 3. After they sin by eating the fruit, they hide from God. By hiding, they are orienting themselves away from God or turning their backs to God. As a result of their actions, they must leave the Garden and for the first-time experience distance from God. In relational terms, we might think of distance as estrangement. The greater the distance, the greater our estrangement from God. The closer the distance, the greater our intimacy with God. Our external sins are brought about by our internal orientation away from God and estrangement from God.

This is why repentance is often described as turning around. It is reorienting ourselves towards God. Repentance does not immediately dispel all the distance between us and God, but it allows us to turn back towards God and sense God's presence.

What is Hell?

Hell is what we experience when our distance from God becomes so great that we cannot sense God no matter where we turn. Think of a hiker lost in wilderness trying to find their way on a pitch-black night with clouds preventing any light from the moon and stars from reaching them. No matter where they look, they can't see the path home.

We experience hell in this life when we spend so much time and energy trying to heal our own wounds and achieve our own goals without God's help that we become completely blind to God's presence and deaf to God's voice – entirely unable to reorient ourselves towards God. While the Bible uses many different analogies for hell including a pit, a place of fire, and a grave, they each describe a place of pure separation from God. Jesus' own teachings warn us that without repentance our temporary experiences in hell during this life could become eternal experiences in the next life.[20]

---

[20] See Matthew 13:36-43.

Our Problem

Confronted with the stark realities of sin and hell, it is easy to revert back to the simple spiritual mindset I displayed as 10-year-old: "This stuff sounds awful! Quick, someone show me how to avoid it, preferably in a few straightforward, easy steps."

Unfortunately, when you are in a place where you cannot see God, feel God, or hear God, there's no quick easy way to repent and turn towards God. On our own, we cannot break through the distance between us and God.

This is why Jesus came as a Savior, not a psychologist. This is why Jesus gave his life for us, rather than giving us five simple steps to mindfulness and tranquility. This is why Jesus told us to take up our crosses and follow him instead of taking out our journals and writing down our current emotional state.

Please do not misinterpret the statements above. I believe Jesus knew all about psychology. In fact, I believe he created it. And I have been helped by psychologists on numerous occasions, both through words spoken directly to me and their writings published for everyone. I just think Jesus came to give us much more than healthy coping mechanisms for life. He came to give us life itself.

On the cross, Jesus took our hell upon himself to

open to us the gates of the heaven God created for us by reorienting us towards God and overcoming the distance between us and our Creator.

Understanding the Experience

In the years after Jesus' death, as more and more people experienced their sins forgiven by Jesus' sacrifice and their lives restored by his ongoing presence through the Holy Spirit, they naturally began to try to describe how his death saved their lives. At first, their explanations were more narrative and less systematic in nature. For this reason, the work of early writers such as the Apostle Paul; Origen of Alexandria – a prominent Christian theologian during the first half of the 3rd Century; and Augustine of Hippo – whose work spanned the last half of the 4th century and the beginning of the 5th century, are often quoted in support of multiple different atonement theories espoused by later theologians.

An Unpayable Debt

The ransom theory of atonement gained prominence in early Christianity thanks in large part to passages in the writings of Origen and Augustine. In the classical version of this theory, humanity became enslaved to the devil through sin. On the cross, Jesus' life served as the necessary ransom payment to set humanity free from the devil's grasp. More contemporary versions of the ransom theory sometimes emphasize Jesus freeing humanity from its enslavement to the powers of sin and death rather than the devil. In either case, with their debt paid, humanity is once again able to experience intimacy with God, to love God and their neighbors wholeheartedly, and to find comfort in the assurance of eternal salvation.

A More Satisfactory Proposal

In 1048, a fifteen-year-old Italian boy from an influential family left home to escape the rule of his overbearing father. As a person of faith endowed with an amazing intellect, he wanted to travel and discover what life had to offer. Following his father's death roughly a decade later, he chose to give up his vast inheritance to become a Benedictine monk, trading monetary wealth for the wealth of intellectual opportunities provided by the monastery. Once there, he quickly distinguished himself through his writings and leadership abilities, eventually resulting in his elevation to the role of Archbishop of Canterbury – an office from which he challenged previous assumptions about the church's leadership structure and feuded with King William II over issues of church and state.

Never one to dream small or back down from his opinions, Anselm of Canterbury – as he came to be known, grew increasingly dissatisfied with the ransom theory of atonement. So, he took it upon himself to write Cur Deus Homo (Why a God Man?), one of the most influential works of theology during the Middle Ages, in which he explored the very nature of God's incarnation in the person of Jesus of Nazareth. In Cur Deus Homo, Anselm articulated his problems with the ransom theory of atonement and proposed an alternative view which came to be known as the satisfaction theory of atonement.

Anselm's problem with the ransom theory of atonement stemmed from his inability to buy into the idea God could owe the devil a ransom. The devil was a creature, a creature God had cursed. God could not owe ransom to a creature. God created humanity and God could do with humanity as God pleased.

The debt sin created was not a debt to the devil. It was a debt humanity owed to God which humanity was entirely incapable of repaying. Through sin, humanity offended God's honor. As a God of justice, God could not simply overlook sin. To do so would be to condone sin, thereby shredding the moral fabric of creation. For humanity to be saved, God had to find a way to carry out justice without destroying the creatures he loved for their rebellion.

The only way God's desire for justice, often termed

God's wrath, could be satisfied would be for a person of absolute innocence and divine perfection to give his life for the sins of humanity. To offer humanity forgiveness and salvation, God the Father would first need to offer up the life of His only begotten Son, who become incarnate as Jesus of Nazareth, the God man.

A Substitute Amendment

Half a millennium later in the midst of the Protestant Reformation, Martin Luther and John Calvin sought to improve upon and expand the satisfaction theory of atonement. They argued sin created a legal dilemma for God. Humanity deserved to be eternally condemned for its sin. In the divine court of law, each person therefore stood under a guilty verdict. When Jesus gave his life on the cross, he was taking upon himself the guilt of humanity and offering his body as a substitute for the punishment humanity deserved. By giving over his body to be abused in humanity's stead, Jesus gained the authority to give humanity his righteousness – his right relationship with God, so that heaven's gates could open and humanity could once again experience intimacy with God.

This theory is generally referred to as the penal substitution theory, though you will sometimes hear versions of it called the vicarious substitution theory or simply substitution theory.

Finding Forgiveness and Freedom

You may recognize the ransom, satisfaction, or substitution theory as the primary way you understand forgiveness and salvation. Or you may be somewhat revolted by the idea of God paying the devil a ransom or the need to satisfy God's wrath. In either case, I'd like to challenge you to consider why it is that these theories of atonement still maintain such a prominent place in the Christian religion after all these centuries. Could it be because they each articulate something true about the nature of our relationship with God?

No Additional Ransom Needed

Whether or not God needed to pay the devil a ransom, we can rest assured – thanks to Jesus' death on the cross – we can no longer be enslaved by the powers of evil and death.

Several years ago, I met a young man who grew up in abject poverty. Joining a gang seemed like a good solution to his teenage mind. In the gang, he found steady income and a family-like atmosphere– at first. As time went on, he realized gang life wasn't going to lead him where he wanted to go. Inevitably he tried to quit, and gang members used intimidation to force him to stay. When I would visit him along with other church leaders interested in helping him get out of the gang, I remember how often he would say, "I can never get out. I just owe them too much."

It reminded me of many conversations I've had with women stuck in abusive relationships. The man in their life pays the bills, but physically and verbally abuses them. The only time he treats them well is right after he has abused them to ensure they won't leave him or call the cops. If they left him, they don't know where they would go or how they would make it on their own. Often, they'll say, "Yes, he's got some big problems. But I owe him a lot."

Young men in gangs and women in abusive relationships need to know they don't owe those who manipulate and abuse them anything. Jesus is more than capable of paying their debts and even taking care of those they must leave behind to find a better life.

While these may be rather dramatic examples, many people find the joy sucked out of life by constantly feeling like we must keep everyone happy. In the psychological realm, this is known as co-dependency. They over-function at home and wonder why no one appreciates them, and then they go to work and compensate for their under-performing co-workers. They need to know they don't owe anyone else happiness, nor are they responsible for what others should do to take care of themselves. They need find their self-worth through

Jesus who sees them as worthy, giving his life for them, and not through thinking they can fix everything for everyone else.

Do you feel like you owe other people or other priorities, a degree of allegiance which should be reserved for God alone? Are there persons or forces in your life asking you to turn away from godly values or from God's call upon your life?

There is a lady in my church named Liz who told me recently that she has discovered a highly effective way to handle struggles and temptations. When those moments arise, she calms herself down and then she tells the devil to "Get off of God's Property." Maybe it's time for you to tell the forces pulling you away from God's dream for your life that thanks to Jesus they no longer have any power over you and they need to get off of God's property!

Struggling to be Satisfied

Have you ever met someone who just couldn't seem to forgive themselves? No matter how much others forgave, they just kept beating themselves up over their mistakes.

If you struggle with perfectionism, you probably know what I'm talking about. You have a very clear idea of exactly how life is supposed to be lived and you are keenly aware of your inability do so. On your good days, you're able to remind yourself no one is perfect, but on your bad days your self-esteem drops like a rock when you make a mistake, and you end up trying to soothe your wounded ego by thinking bad thoughts about other people and reminding yourself how much better you are than them.

Or maybe you've got something in your past which you just can't get over. You know you made some dumb decisions. You know you hurt a lot of people. You've taken responsibility and admitted there was no one to blame but yourself. And now you're stuck, unable to blame others for your problems and unable to get out from under the unbearable shame you feel.

In either case, you might well resort to berating yourself over your shortcomings in the hope that eventually you will beat yourself up so much God and others will take pity on you and forgive you. It's as if you have become your own arresting officer, prosecutor, judge, jury, and jailer. Though you are rightly searching for forgiveness, you never seem to find it because you are operating under the false assumption you can somehow punish yourself enough to earn it. So, you continue to live in a more or less constant internal state of self-loathing and shame, no matter how well life is going on the outside.

You need to know that on the cross, Jesus satisfied the wrath of God. Jesus did not allow his body to be beaten on the cross so that you would need to beat yourself up for your sins. Jesus died so that you could stop beating yourself up and receive the undeserved forgiveness he offers. Maybe it's time for you to stop trying to earn the gift of Jesus' grace, and instead just accept it and begin living out of your gratitude for it.

Sometimes You Need a Sub

It's difficult for some people to fathom why humanity deserves judgment or why Jesus would need to take upon himself the punishment we deserve. For others, it's much easier.

Currently, I have the privilege of being friends with a number of people who, sadly, have first- hand experience with violence. Some of them got involved in violent confrontations as the result of poor choices, others did so due to the influence of alcohol or drugs. Tragically, some of them have even taken life. As I have sat in Bible studies with them, be it in a cramped church Sunday school room or on the other side of reinforced plexiglass at the nearby prison, I have always been struck by how well they relate to the substitution theory of atonement.

I think especially of one man who would hold out his massive hands in front of him and say, "When I think about what these hands did to my wife and children when I was drinking, I cry out, 'Why, God, why? Why did you let me bruise my wife? Why did you let my kids grow up in fear of their dad? Why didn't you just let me overdose and be done with it? Why did you let me hurt them so badly?'"

He knows all too well the consequences of his actions and he knows what he deserves as a result his sins. When he sees Jesus on the cross, he knows he should be the one hanging there. To know that Jesus, the only one his actions hurt worse than his wife and kids, would give his life for him is about the only thing he can imagine which could possibly give him another chance at peace and happiness, much less salvation. As he once told me, "The only way I can sleep at night is knowing not only did Jesus suffer so I could be forgiven, he's willing to suffer anything it takes so my wife and kids can find healing."

Your story may be very different from the story of my friend who found sobriety too late in life to save his marriage or salvage his relationship with his kids. However, I imagine if you take an honest appraisal of your life you wouldn't want to receive what you deserve for the passive aggressive ways you have used sharp words to wound others deeply, the times when you intentionally manipulated people in pursuit of selfish gain, and those moments no one knows about when you declined to help those in need because it was too inconvenient.

There are times when we all need to look at the cross and know Jesus went there so we wouldn't have to.

Heaven and a Hell of a Question

Please permit me to ask you one final question before we move to other ways of understanding how Jesus' death puts us at one with God: Do you have an assurance of your salvation?

Have you felt God forgiving your sins and removing them from you as far as the east is from the west? Do you know Jesus has prepared a place for you in the eternal glory of his Father's Kingdom? If following Christ faithfully meant literally laying down your earthly life, could you do so in the confidence that you would be with Christ that very day in paradise?

If so, are you living in the peace and joy that assurance brings? Are you forgiving others as you have been forgiven? Or are you slipping back into old patterns of trying to build your self-worth upon your own accomplishments and skills, and defining yourself by looking down on others and thinking how much better you are than they? Don't slip back into slavery after you have been set free.

If you have not experienced an assurance of salvation, I want you to know you don't have to live the rest of your life that way – wondering if God is real, wondering if you'll go to the good place or the bad place or any place at all when you die. The Bible teaches us when we invite Jesus into our lives his Holy Spirit gives us an assurance of his presence and of our salvation. Keep praying to Christ and trust he will answer, in his way, in his time, in a far more powerful manner than you could ever imagine.

I'm guessing some of you have prayed many times for forgiveness and salvation, but you have never felt that overpowering moment. That's okay. For some of us, it's an emotional experience with tears and sobs. For others, it's a very quiet internal sense of confidence which comes over us. This is how it was the famous Christian author, C.S. Lewis, who described his conversion as occurring while riding a motorcycle on a trip to the local zoo. When he began the journey, he was unsure of his religious beliefs. And though there was not an especially miraculous moment during the journey, by the time he arrived at the zoo, he somehow knew beyond a shadow of a doubt Jesus was the Son of God.

It may even be you have prayed to give your life to Jesus and heard God saying to you what God said to me years ago: Wait. If this is the case for you, then wait for your experience in the knowledge that while you wait you are being held in the secure arms of a God who paid the highest price on the cross so that no power in heaven or hell could steal you from His embrace.

CHAPTER THREE
The Great War

During the dark days of apartheid in South Africa, protesters assembled for a rally at St. George's Cathedral in Cape Town. As Archbishop Desmond Tutu addressed the crowd, state police, intent on shutting down the gathering, entered the sanctuary and surrounded the participants. Facing the prospect of being forcefully dispersed and seeing their leaders arrested, nervous murmurs spread throughout the crowd.

As the tension in the room reached its crescendo, Bishop Tutu veered from his prepared remarks to address the police force directly. "You are powerful," he told the police. "But God is more powerful. And God cannot be mocked. You have already lost. Therefore, since you have lost, we are inviting you to join the winning side."

Stunned by his words, the crowd erupted with cheers and dancing. Equally stunned by the bravado of the

Bishop, the police withdrew, allowing the celebration to spill out of the church and into the streets.

We now know the rest of the story. Several years later, under mounting pressure from internal protests and international condemnation, South Africa's apartheid regime fell, ushering in a new democratic government intent on leading the country through the hard work of inclusion and reconciliation. But Bishop Tutu did not know the end of the story when he opened his arms to extend an unexpected invitation to the armed police surrounding him. So how did he know he was on the winning side? Was he bluffing? Were his words just an example of wishful thinking which by chance came true? Or, as a follower of a crucified Savior, did he know something about the nature of the world that supporters of apartheid failed to grasp?

Rethinking Ransom

In 1930, Gustaf Aulén, a professor of systematic theology at Lund University in Sweden, published *The Christian Idea of Atonement.* A year later, his book was translated into English and given a new title, *Christus Victor.*

In Christus Victor, Aulén argued later Christian theologians, including Anselm, misinterpreted the writings of earlier Christian leaders such as Origen and

Augustine. Rather than the early church subscribing primarily to the ransom theory of atonement in which Jesus must pay the devil's ransom with his death to free the souls of humanity from hell, Aulén claimed the early church believed Jesus' died on the cross to defeat the cosmic powers sin, death, and devil. Instead of paying the devil off, Jesus's death served as a full-frontal assault on the devil and all the forces of sin and evil. Jesus' victory in this battle against evil stripped the devil of any further power to enslave humanity to sin.

Furthermore, in contrast to the Anselm's satisfaction theory of atonement, the **Christus Victor theory of atonement** saw Jesus' death not as satisfying God's wrath in a legal sense, but rather as God Himself winning the decisive battle to liberate humanity from its enslavement to sin. Just as the waters sweeping back across the Red Sea to drown the Egyptian army marked the definitive victory which set the Hebrews free under Moses' leadership, so the definitive victory over evil and sin occurred when clouds swept in to cover the sky and Jesus cried out from the cross: "It is finished!"[21] – a shout of victory in the war against evil, not of resignation to a humiliating death.

So persuasive were Aulén's historical and theological theses that 1900 years after Jesus' death, Christus Victor transformed widely held assumptions about the

---

[21] John 19:30

meaning of the cross and the history of the early church for large swaths of Christians, especially within Protestant traditions. Perhaps the Christus Victor theory of atonement gained tractions so quickly in Christian theology because Christians immediately recognized its congruence with the focus of Jesus' life and ministry.

Battling from the Beginning

Jesus' earthly life begins with a direct confrontation with the worst evil humanity has to offer. Shortly after Jesus' birth, King Herod learns of a child born in Bethlehem who is prophesied to be the future King of the Jews. Herod, having no intention of giving up his place as the King of the Jews without a fight, sends troops to Bethlehem with orders to kill all young male babies. Jesus' family escapes the massacre by fleeing to Egypt by night, while many other families were not so lucky. Following Herod's death several years later, Jesus' family returned from Egypt, settling in Nazareth in order to escape any lingering suspicion that making their home in Bethlehem might have engendered.

Similarly, Jesus' public ministry begins with a direct confrontation with cosmic evil and the devil. Our first account of Jesus' adult life occurs when he travels to the Jordan River to be baptized by John the Baptist. In a seemingly made-for-television moment, just as Jesus is coming out of the water, the clouds part, the Holy Spirit descends from the sky in the form of a dove, and a voice from heaven booms, "This is my Son, the Beloved, with whom I am well pleased."[22]

Immediately thereafter, the Holy Spirit whisks Jesus away from this glorious celebration at the river and leads Jesus to the wilderness where he will fast for 40 days and 40 nights before being tempted by the devil. Taking advantage of Jesus' weakened physical condition from his days of fasting, the devil presents Jesus with the greatest temptations possible.[23]

First, the devil instructs Jesus to turn stones into bread. Jesus had the power to do it. He could satisfy his hunger and even create enough extra food to feed all the hungry people in the world. All Jesus had to do was to take matters into his own hands rather than trusting God the Father to provide. Of course, Jesus says no.

Next, the devil took Jesus to the top of the temple in Jerusalem and begins to hypothesize about what would happen if Jesus threw himself off the temple, knowing the angels would catch him on the way down. Everyone would see it. It would be the biggest thing since sliced bread. Wait – there was no sliced bread back then. It would be the biggest thing ever! Instant fame and celebrity awaited. Everyone would follow him. No one

---

[22] Matthew 3:17 (NRSV)

[23] Matthew 4:1-11

would be able to deny his power and divinity. You know what happens next. Jesus gives the devil a hard pass. Divinity was not designed for magic shows.

Finally, the devil shows Jesus the view on a high mountaintop from which he could see all the kingdoms of the earth. All these kingdoms, the devil would give to him, if only he would turn his back on God the Father and worship the devil. Unlimited power was at his fingertips. He could set up the perfect government with the perfect policies and the perfect religion and the perfect economy for everyone everywhere in the world. Sounds good. Given the state of politics today, you may find yourself secretly wishing Jesus had given in.

Utopia within grasp. One nation under... And there's the catch. It wouldn't be one nation under God, it would be one nation under the devil. God gave humanity free will to love their creator or to turn away from His ways. The devil would strip their free will and allow Jesus the power to make humanity his puppets.

No dice. Jesus tells the devil to go back where he came from; and Jesus' temptations come to an end, for the moment.

Final Verse Same as the First

In Jesus' last days, he once again finds himself locked in a battle with the vilest evil human politics can concoct and the cosmic consequences of the devil's temptations.

As Jesus' influence grew among the people, the Jewish political and religious leaders became increasingly threatened by his unwillingness to subscribe to all their policies and submit to their authority. Eventually, they came to fear he could de-legitimize their entire power structure with his subversive tendencies and seemingly self-appointed authority to reinterpret scripture.

The Jewish leaders, most likely, would have disposed of Jesus more quickly except for his incredible popularity with the people. His care for each person, the healings he worked, and his breathtaking teachings led him to become Judaism's most esteemed religious leader in the eyes of the common people, though certainly not from the viewpoint of the elite.

Eventually, the Jewish leaders started efforts to quiet Jesus and undermine his authority by trapping him with unanswerable questions. Yet, each time they did so, Jesus came up with the perfect response which publicly embarrassed the Jewish leaders and further endeared himself to the masses. Once these milder tactics had been proven ineffective, there was only one option left. Jesus had to be eliminated.

Taking Jesus out would require a clever and complex operation. If they tried to do it themselves, they could run afoul of the Roman law. If they captured Jesus in broad daylight, the crowds supporting him might rise up and overpower them. They had to find a way to end Jesus' life while also undermining his popularity with the people.

They came up with the perfect plan. They would capture him by night while most of the Jerusalem slept. Hold a trial for blasphemy in the wee hours of the mornings. Convict him based on his habit of forgiving sins and a few of his other teachings that seemed to indicate he believed himself to have power beyond what is natural for humans. Then, they would turn him over to the Roman governor to be crucified by their gentile rulers as a rebel threatening the stability of the empire by claiming to be the Messiah, the King of the Jews.

If everything went according to plan, the people would turn on Jesus. When they saw he was just like all the others who had gotten their hopes up for restored Jewish political sovereignty – claiming to be the long-awaited Messiah before being defeated and killed by the Romans – the people would turn on him. Instead of looking upon him as a wise rabbi, the people would have no choice but to see him as a threat to provoke Rome to further oppress and terrorize the entire Jewish population. The prophecy which caused King Herod to seek his life as a child would now be the charge brought against him at the trial for his life.

It all worked like a charm. So thoroughly did the people turn against Jesus that when the only hiccup in the plan occurred– and the Roman Governor, Pontius Pilate, found Jesus innocent of all charges– the people cried out with such fervor for Jesus to be crucified that Pilate went along with it simply to appease them.

This is how it came to be that Jesus, the only completely innocent person in human history, was tortured and nailed to a cross thanks to a shrewd political power play executed by the Jewish religious leaders in unison with the most powerful government on earth for the sake of maintaining the status quo power structure.

The Ultimate Temptation

The Gospel of Luke tells us after the devil unsuccessfully tempted Jesus in the wilderness, the devil "departed from him until a more opportune time."[24] Strangely, the devil never reappears to tempt Jesus in Luke's Gospel. How could the author of Luke, who by his own admission investigated the stories of Jesus meticulously and sought to write "an orderly account"[25] of Jesus' life, fail to report the devil's reappearance at a more opportune time which he explicitly foreshadowed?

Perhaps Luke expected the reader to understand

---

[24] Luke 4:13

[25] Luke 1:3

the temptations to avoid suffering and death which Jesus experienced while praying in the Garden of Gethsemane and while hanging on the cross were all of the devil's design. Wasn't it Jesus himself who had referred to Peter as Satan for the mere suggestion that Jesus should be spared suffering and death?[26] Yet, here was Jesus in the garden shortly before his arrest so perplexed by his desire to avoid suffering that his sweat became like drops of blood as he prayed.[27] And there was Jesus on the cross listening to the crowd taunt him with the ultimate temptation: "If you are the King of the Jews, save yourself!"[28]

It's not hard at all to recognize the devil's design in the nature of the temptations. Just as he was in the wilderness, on the cross Jesus is tempted to betray the fundamental nature of God while in a weakened physical condition. You might even say on the cross God was tempted to betray His own nature and succumb to the devil's ways. It seemed the devil would win no matter what. Either Jesus would betray God's nature by using his divine power for selfish gain or Jesus would die and the devil would have free reign again on earth.

The devil may not have been the only one hoping

---

[26] Matthew 16:23

[27] Luke 22:44

[28] Luke 23:37

Jesus would come off the cross. Surely Jesus' followers, who had seen him perform miracles day after day were hoping against hope he would perform one final miracle by calling down an army of angels to take him off the cross and show his enemies who was really in charge.

I have an image in my mind – though you should know it appears only in my head and cannot be found in scripture – of an angel army hovering in the air just above the cross invisible to all but Jesus. Row upon row of angels with flaming swords and chariots of fire. A greater military force than has ever been or will ever be assembled by the nations on earth; waiting for the command to invade, to rescue Jesus, and defeat his tormentors. Each angel eagerly watching the archangels at the front of the formation for the command they all knew was coming.

I envision the archangels calling out to Jesus, begging for the command to unleash the fury of heaven on the devil's accomplices. Then I see the archangels with horror in their eyes realizing the command will never come. Gradually their horror turns to sadness and their sadness to awe.

One by one, beginning with the archangels, the angels sheath their swords, remove their helmets, bend low on one knee, and bow their heads before the divine Son of God. At that moment, the angels realized what the world would have to wait for Jesus' resurrection to discover: on the cross they were not witnessing Jesus' collapse, but rather his coronation.

Through giving his life on the cross for his Jewish betrayers and his Gentile tormentors, the man convicted of claiming to be King of the Jews became not only King of the Jews, but King of the world. While the kings and kingdoms of Jesus' day are now mostly footnotes in the annals of history, he remains the most read about, most talked about, most influential figure in all of history.

The forces of evil conspired to do their worst and they were resoundingly defeated by a crucified Jewish rabbi with only a few followers who remained faithful until the bitter end. On the cross, Jesus won the battle for the very nature of God. God is love, sacrificial love with no end, and God will always be love. His death is the guarantee that contrary to popular opinion, sacrificial love will always be the most powerful force moving history forward.

Why Does It Even Matter?

You might be wondering what the big deal is about Jesus' defeat of evil. Even if it's true, what difference does it really make for our daily living? Sure, some of you may have loved imagining the cosmic battle between good and evil taking place as Jesus hung on the cross, though I imagine some of the less religiously-minded among you may have heard the story of the angel armies and thought: this feels like a cheesy low budget Easter movie.

I do not believe there is any more crucial event for determining how we live our lives than Jesus' death on the cross. We still live in a world in which the devil's temptations are all too real. You do not have to look far to see unethical business practices rewarded with ungodly wealth, military might stealing the people's right to determine their own method of government, and growing divisions based on race, religion, and resources.

In such a world, we are all faced with the question: What really makes a difference? And in such a world, we are all confronted with the devil's temptations to deploy evil means to accomplish a good agenda. It's a fool's game the devil invites us to play, yet many of us can't seem to resist playing it again and again – though we end up losing every time.

I've actually had church people tell me that Jesus' ways of treating people only work in spiritual matters. In the real world, they assure me, you can't live by Jesus' ethics or you'll get nowhere.

The fact is, these well-meaning church folks would be absolutely right if Jesus had called down the angels to take him off the cross and slaughter his enemies. But he didn't. And because he didn't, we know what really makes a difference: sacrificial love. Scheming, cheating, oppressing, and manipulating all these tactics lead not to victory but defeat, no matter how promising their immediate results seem.

Beams of Heaven

In 1906, Charles Albert Tindley penned "Beams of Heaven as I Go." Born in 1851, the free son of a slave father and free mother, Tindley educated himself and eventually became an ordained minister in the Methodist Episcopal Church. He led his church in Philadelphia to become a multiracial congregation numbering more than 10,000. From his experience growing up surrounded by slavery in his childhood and seeing the ongoing oppression of blacks in Northern cities during his adult years, Tindley penned these words:

> *Harder yet may be the fight;*
> *right may often yield to might;*
> *wickedness a while may reign;*
> *Satan's cause may seem to gain.*
> *There is a God that rules above,*
> *with hand of power and heart of love;*
> *if I am right, he'll fight my battle,*
> *I shall have peace someday.*[29]

---

[29] Charles Albert Tindley. "Beams of Heaven as I Go." See https://hymnary.org/hymn/UMH/524. Accessed November 11, 2020.

Tindley was right. There are times when the direction of history can seem ambiguous, and we must look to the cross to remind ourselves where the victory is found. If we fail to remember how Jesus won the victory over the devil, we will inevitably succumb to the devil's temptations to use evil methods to accomplish good, just as many of our well-meaning Christian ancestors did.

When Good People Do Bad Things

Just three centuries after Jesus was crucified by the Roman empire's soldiers, Christianity became the empire's official religion. Not long thereafter, Christian leaders sent out Roman soldiers to threaten pagan tribes with death if they chose not to convert to the religion of the crucified Savior. Today, it's easy to wonder how they could possibly do such a thing. Yet, from their writings, it is apparent they really thought God was using them to bring the whole world to Christ through their actions. In fact, the devil was using them to undermine the spiritual authority of the church.

Before the 1400s, racism as we know it today did not exist. Of course, people still struggled with tribalism and prejudice, but they did not base their prejudice purely on skin color until two discoveries changed all that.

When European powers, representing some of the most Christian societies on earth, discovered sailing routes to the West Coast of Africa and the new American continents, a deadly combination emerged. On Africa's West Coast, vast numbers of slaves could be captured or purchased for a relatively low cost, while the new American continents provided an untold wealth of natural resources, if only the colonizers could acquire the cheap labor needed to harvest them.

It was this promise of the unimaginable wealth which could be acquired through a free labor force that led European politicians and philosophers to create the cruelest form of slavery in recorded history and to justify it by claiming those with darker skin were created by God to be subservient to those of lighter skin. Within this period, there were some Christian leaders who stood up against these obviously heretical views. Sadly, there were many more who wholeheartedly went along with them. Self-interest is a horrifyingly powerful force and Christians are by no means immune to it.

I can trace one line of my own family lineage to white slave-owners who farmed large plantations in Alabama. Many wonderful stories come from this particular branch of my family tree; stories of ingenuity, prioritizing education, and sincere Christian faith. And yet! They were simultaneously engaged in one of the vilest, most morally disgraceful practices the world has ever known.

Less than a century after the abolition of slavery in the United States, my maternal grandfather, the grandson of slave owners, shipped off to the European theater of World War II. In his role as a surgeon, he saw first-hand the horror wrought upon the world by Nazi Germany as he tried his best to put back together young men who had been ripped apart by their bullets and bombs.

Only after returning home would he, along with the rest of the country, learn the full depth of Nazi atrocities. Germany, regarded as one of the most educated Christian nations on earth, had developed and implemented a systematic plan to murder the entire Jewish population along with other people groups they deemed undeserving of a place in society. While Adolf Hitler could be described at most as a nominal Christian, many sincere German Christians wholeheartedly went along with his schemes.[30]

Charles Albert Tindley was right. There are moments when "Satan's cause may seem to gain."

Thankfully, his next verse is also right. "There is a God who rules above with hand of power and heart of love."

---

[30] If you are wondering why I have only highlighted atrocities committed from within the Christian tradition in this section, you are right to note history finds atrocities in almost all secular societies and faith traditions. I have noted Christian failures in these pages to demonstrate the devil's ability to convince even the followers of the crucified Lord to adopt evil ways.

The Difference the Cross Makes for Daily Living

In our daily living, we do well to remember the truth of Jesus' victory over evil and death articulated in Tindley's lyrics. There will often be times when following the ways of Jesus, the ways of sacrificial love, will lead to short term loss. In these moments, we should not neglect Jesus' ways for they are, in fact, the only ways that lead to long-term gain.

Consider the life of Anjezë Gonxhe Bojaxhiu, who you probably know as Mother Teresa. A nun, enjoying the privileged life of a teacher within the confines of her convent in Calcutta, she could not rid herself of the thought of the suffering occurring just outside its walls. After years of lobbying her superiors, she was allowed to venture outside the convent's walls to minister to the poor of the city. With no resources at her disposal, she was forced to beg for food for herself and those for whom she cared. At the time, many people criticized her for being naive enough to try to tackle such a massive problem with such meager resources. Today, the way the poor and the dying are treated throughout the world has been transformed by her example. The world is a more compassionate place because she chose the way of sacrificial love.

In our country, Rev. Dr. Martin Luther King, Jr. called for civil rights based on Jesus' love for all.

Though he was the target of significant criticism from within the black community for calling them to love and seek the best for their white oppressors while other voices were calling for violent uprisings, Dr. King's example remains the vision we look to in times of division and discord.

Do not be deceived. History is moved forward by sacrificial love. And not just by sacrificial love on the part of people who will become famous. History is moved forward by every small act of sacrificial love.

A few years ago, I was part of a church with an ongoing ministry partnership in El Salvador. Several times a year, we would send a team to work under the guidance of local church leaders with the people of a small village building church facilities, leading Bible school for the children, providing a free medical clinic, and visiting the people in their homes. It did not take long for the doctors running the medical clinic to identify the lack of clean drinking water as the greatest health problem facing the community.

For quite some time, the residents of the village had been petitioning the government to run water lines from the nearby city up to the village with no apparent success. Eventually, the engineers in our church got tired of waiting for the El Salvadorian government to do what everyone knew needed to be done. So, they began dreaming up, designing, and raising money for a rainwater catchment system that would provide clean drinking water for the village, at least during the wet season.

Many people criticized this initiative as seeking to do for the people of the village what their government should do for them instead. But when you see the same kids malnourished and sick year after year, it just does something to you. Accordingly, our engineers ignored the critics and pressed on with their project.

Eventually, the system was installed. Then, just as it was about to be put into use, large government trucks rumbled into the village to run water lines. The government did not want the church to be seen as doing the job the government was supposed to do for the people. So, while the catchment system never came fully online, it more than accomplished its purpose of bringing clean water to the village.

Christ the Victor

Let me ask you a question: Are you living as if Jesus Christ won the definitive victory over evil on the cross?

Or do you live as if believing in Jesus will get you to heaven when you die, but following his ways here and now will get you nowhere fast?

Are there places in your life where you've adopted the ways and means of the devil because you were afraid of the short-term loss you might endure if you followed the ways of Jesus?

What would it look like for you to embrace Jesus' ways in every area of your life?

Who would you have to forgive? What amends would you need to make? Are there habits you would need to break? Business practices that need to be changed? Relationships that need more time and attention?

Living a life of sacrificial love right here, right now, may seem quite scary. It may also be the only way to live a life with lasting significance.

The Great War

Before World War II began, World War I was generally called The Great War. It was also commonly known as The War to End All Wars. People believed after seeing the horrors of The Great War, humanity would never again enter into such a conflict. Of course, they were wrong. The treaty ending World War I sowed the seeds of World War II. War can't end war – only sacrificial love can.

On the cross, Jesus triumphed in the great war over evil by refusing to call down the angel armies and voluntarily suffering for the sins of humanity. Ever since, there has been no question about who wins in the end: sacrificial love wins. And one day God's eternal kingdom of sacrificial love will be the only kingdom left standing.

Is today the day for you to join the winning side?

CHAPTER FOUR
A New Nature

Have you ever noticed how much easier it is to know the right thing to do, than to do it?

You know you should get eight hours of sleep a night, but it's just so nice to stay up and watch television.

You know you should order the salad, but the Philly cheese steak and fries are so good at this place.

Every time you have more than one drink in public you say or do something you regret, but you're having a great time. One more drink couldn't possibly hurt that much, could it?

You know you should exercise for 30 minutes a day, but you don't want to get out of bed a half-hour early, and by the time you get off work, you're so tired you don't feel like stopping at the gym on the way home.

Should I go on? I can. You know I can. Because you can. We all can.

Everyone knows the best of intentions do not always lead to any significant actions. Knowing the right thing to do and doing it are two very different things.

The Old Self

As hard as it was for early church leaders to convince a skeptical public of Jesus' resurrection from the dead in the first decades after his death, they found it even harder to get those who came to believe in Jesus to live by Jesus' teachings.

Writing to the fledgling church at Ephesus, the Apostle Paul felt compelled to remind its members:

> *You were taught to put away your former way of life, your old self, corrupt and deluded by its lusts, and to be renewed in the spirit of your minds, and to clothe yourselves with the new self, created according to the likeness of God in true righteousness and holiness.* [31]

I often refer to my old self, before I came to faith in Christ, as the old boy. I do not refer to him as the old man because there was not much mature about him. Sure, he had a lot going for him - as is the case for all of us who are created in the image of God. He authentically wanted to be a good person. He was smart, though far from wise. And he had a lot of passion. But the old boy was dominated by lusts: lust for acceptance, lust

---
[31] Ephesians 4:22-24

for status, lust for money, lust for sex, lust for whatever success looked like at that particular moment.

When I accepted Christ, I became a new man. My heart genuinely changed. I no longer wanted to treat others well simply so people would think I was a good person. I wanted to treat others well because of how inconceivably well Jesus treated me. My understanding of success changed almost overnight from being about how much I could get to being about how much I could give.

With Jesus in the driver's seat, everything changed. I was a new person. Except the old boy didn't go away entirely. He just switched seats. Now he's that guy who tries to navigate from the passenger seat regardless of whether he actually knows where he is going or not.

There are few things which make me madder than when I am driving in heavy traffic through unfamiliar territory and the person in the passenger seat, who is supposed to be navigating for me, gets distracted by the scenery and loses track of where we are and where we need to turn next. This is the role the old boy plays in my life twenty-four hours a day seven days a week. He's always got advice to share about how I should live my life, most of it unhelpful. With Jesus' help, I've spent the last several decades of my life learning how to ignore his incorrect directions. Needless to say, I've still got a lot of learning to do.

One of the leaders of our church's recovery ministry with several decades of sobriety under his belt makes a habit of repeatedly telling the men around him: "The same man will drink again." He is trying to impress upon them it's not enough just to decide that giving up alcohol is the right thing to do. If your decision is the only thing keeping you sober, you won't be sober long. Temptation will sneak up on you and you'll give in. If you want to stay sober, something on the inside must change. You must become a new person.

Becoming Christ-like

Taken together the ransom, satisfaction, substitution, and Christus Victor theories of atonement do a good job of articulating how we can find forgiveness, salvation, and confidence in the power of good to triumph over evil through Jesus Christ's death and resurrection. They say relatively little, however, about how we can become like Christ on the inside. To truly be at one with God, it is not enough simply to believe in Jesus' divinity and receive his gifts. We must be transformed into his image.

In the latter half of the second century, Irenaeus of Lyons, a Greek Bishop in what is now France, turned his attention to a simple question: How does the cross make us like Christ? His answer came to be known as the **recapitulation theory of atonement.**

According to Irenaeus' articulation of the recapitulation theory, the image of God in which humanity was created became distorted after Adam sinned, leaving humanity no possible way to regain the intimacy with God Adam enjoyed in the garden of Eden. In Jesus' life, death, and resurrection, Irenaeus saw Jesus functioning as the second Adam who, unlike the original Adam, remained faithful in the face of temptation. By doing so, Jesus offered humanity what they could not acquire otherwise – the chance to have the image of God restored within them and once again experience intimacy with God by becoming like Christ.

In Irenaeus' view, Jesus "became what we are, that He might bring us to be even what He is Himself."[32]

While the recapitulation theory of atonement became quite influential in the eastern church, western expressions of Christianity never granted it the same position of prominence. As a result, centuries later western theologians, taking notice of the lack of focus on personal transformation in the dominant atonement theories of their day, also sought to explain how Jesus' death offered humanity the chance to become Christ-like as Irenaeus had done in his day.

---

[32] Irenaeus, *Against Heresies, Preface to Book 5* in A. Roberts and J. Donaldson (eds), *The Writings of Irenaeus Vol. 2* (Edinburgh: T & T Clark, 1869), p. 55.

The Ultimate Influencer

Living around the turn of the 12th century when Anselm's satisfaction theory came to dominate western ideas about atonement, Peter Abelard, a French philosopher and theologian, responded by offering his own ideas on atonement which we now label as the **moral influence theory of atonement.**

Abelard rejected the idea that God's wrath needed to be satisfied, which was so central to Anselm's satisfaction theory of atonement. If God is unchanging, how could God's mind suddenly change about whether a sinner is worthy of acceptance simply because that sinner suddenly comes to believe in Jesus, Abelard wondered.

When Abelard looked at the cross, he saw the greatest imaginable depth of love. This sacrificial divine love, he believed, was what the cross was all about – showing humanity God was not full of judgment and wrath. Rather, God's nature was full of loving kindness and grace.

How could the image of God be restored in humanity, if humanity fundamentally misunderstood God's nature? According to the moral influence theory of atonement, humanity could never become like Christ until they came to see God as full of grace and love, instead of wrath and vengeance.

From the very beginning, Abelard's teachings were both influential and controversial. So controversial, in fact, that he was nearly excommunicated for his unconventional views. Nevertheless, the strength of his ideas spoke for themselves. Even with the church actively working to silence his voice, Abelard's ideas about atonement continued to influence generations of theologians and eventually gained prominence in some streams of Protestantism.

Whether you agree with Abelard's complete rejection of satisfaction theory or not, his moral influence theory offers up a question which everyone seeking to follow in the ways of Jesus must ask: What is the nature of the God in whose image I have been made? Or, to put it another way: What is my vision of the Christ I am trying to become like?

Leading by Example

Writing almost 500 years after Abelard's heyday, Faustus Socinus, an Italian theologian with a similar willingness to consider ideas outside of the mainstream, began to build on the moral influence theory with teachings which would eventually come to be known as the **moral example theory of atonement**.

While the moral influence theory focused primarily on understanding the nature of God through Jesus' sacrifice on the cross, the moral example theory looks to Jesus' life and death as an example of how we should live our lives. On the cross, Jesus shows us not only how God loves us, but also how we are called to love one another.

The idea we should love one another as Christ has loved us may appear fairly obvious to you. Unfortunately, it hasn't always appeared so to many Christians.

Once after a sermon on loving our neighbors, a church member grabbed me on the way out of church to tell me I was wrong to preach that Jesus wanted us to love everyone as we love ourselves. Instead, he argued Jesus only wanted us to love fellow Christians in that manner. God doesn't love non-Christians as much as God loves Christians, he told me.

When I pressed him as to why we should withhold care from certain people groups when Jesus ministered to Gentiles as well as Jews, he responded that Jesus was trying to save their souls. If we were to extend compassion to them today, we would run the risk of falsely leading them to believe they were already saved.

Instead of seeking to meet the needs of non-Christians as Jesus did for Gentiles through his healings and teachings, this man felt we needed to put all our efforts into ensuring non-Christians understood the judgment and wrath of God they would face unless they came to believe like we did.

Sadly, this man's views were not just an isolated case. In modern-day Protestantism, many more conservative churches, which focus entirely on the substitutionary theory of atonement, often fail to adequately emphasize the need to derive our ethics from Jesus' example since their main emphasis is on escaping condemnation. On the other hand, more liberal Protestant churches subscribing primarily to the moral influence and moral example views of atonement often spend most of their energy encouraging their followers to be good people while leaving them without clear guidance about how to share their faith with nonbelievers and experience forgiveness, the assurance of salvation, and the power of the Holy Spirit living inside them.

Made New

So how do we actually change and become something new?

In the polarized world in which we live, how can we become not a more conservative Christian or a more liberal Christian, but a more Christ-like Christian?

A few years ago, I spoke with a friend who was quite overweight. For as long as he could remember, he had used comfort food as an emotional coping mechanism. As a teenager, he burned off the calories as quickly as he consumed them while running for the high school track team. When his high school track career ended, his eating habits remained the same. By the time he turned 40, he had long given up on being able to live an active lifestyle. His doctor told him all his numbers were headed in the wrong direction. His kids begged him to play with them, but he rarely had the energy. His wife secretly worried about what she would do if he died young.

Every January he'd decide to be healthier. One year, he tried a fad diet. It lasted about a week. The next year, he got a gym membership. This time he went for a month before becoming embarrassed by the way he looked compared to the skinny people on the treadmills beside him. I didn't hold out much hope for him getting healthier.

Then one day I saw him, and he looked healthier and lighter. A couple of months later, he looked even better. When I asked him what happened, his eyes lit up and he replied, "I made a decision."

I pressed him for more info. "Yeah, I know, but you made a lot of decisions in the past. And they didn't work out so well. What was different about this decision?"

"In the past" he said, "I made decisions to lose weight and get healthier and I never did either. This time I decided I was still an athlete. I just needed to rescue my inner athlete from all the excess weight which was robbing me of my athleticism. So, I did what any athlete would do. I joined a team, got a coach, and I even got a sports psychologist to help me manage my anxiety without overeating."

"You worked with a sports psychologist?" I asked incredulously. "I didn't even know there were sports psychologists around here."

"Well, she's not technically a sports psychologist." He admitted. "Her business card just says psychologist. But since she is working with me and I'm an athlete, in my mind that makes her a sports psychologist."

Today my friend is healthier, lighter, and faster than he ever thought he would be again. He's got energy for his family and his doctor refers to him as a success story.

What made the difference?

I believe there were three things my friend did differently this time around which made all the difference.

First, he got a new identity. During unsuccessful attempts to lose weight, his identity was an overweight person trying to lose weight. This time his identity became an athlete getting back into top condition.

There's a lot more power in understanding your identity as being an athlete rather than as an overweight person. Externally, both might have been true. In fact, from the outside looking in no one would have called him an athlete at all. But identity isn't external. It's internal. And once you embrace your identity on the inside it has the power to change a lot on the outside.

Next, he got a new vision. Initially, his vision was to be somewhat thinner, somewhat healthier, and somewhat more energetic. Such a vague uninspiring vision was never going to get him very far. So, he came up with a new one: to be fast.

You can debate what it means to be fast. If you lined up against my friend in a 5K this weekend, you might not consider him super-fast. Of course, he doesn't care what you think is fast. He gets to define fast for himself, and according to his definition, he is fast and getting faster.

Lastly, he got new habits to go along with his new identity and new vision. An athlete getting back in top condition doesn't eat anything they want anytime they want, so he quit doing so. Someone trying to get fast doesn't sleep in till the last possible moment every morning, so he gets up early to run with his teammates.

Now that he has a new lifestyle, he can't imagine going back to the way he used to live. Sure, he doesn't eat kale salad for lunch every day and occasionally he misses a run, though not as often as you might think.

A New Identity

Like my friend who was seeking physical transformation, if we want spiritual transformation to make us more like Christ, we need a new identity. The recapitulation theory of atonement offers us just that.

Thanks to the truth Irenaeus gleaned so many centuries ago, we know our identity as children of God created in the image of God. Yes, sin has distorted God's image in us just as excess weight had distorted my friend's athleticism. But sin has not destroyed it.

We are not hopeless sinners, forever condemned to give in to our worst temptations and separated from the intimacy with God we crave. We are hopeful sinners, children of God growing closer to our Father day-by-day through the gift of atonement given to us by our Savior.

Often in this life, we do experience an intimate connection with God. We may never earn it and it certainly doesn't occur every single day. Nonetheless, it does happen. It's a gift God gives people like us, God's children.

A New Vision

Of course, a new identity will change little about your life without a new vision to go with it. In my friend's case, once he discovered his new identity as an athlete, he had to define his vision of an athlete. He had several options to choose from. He could have defined being an athlete as being strong (which he already was) or he could have defined it as having good hand-eye coordination (which he already had). Pursuing either of these alternative visions might have been enjoyable, but they probably would not have led him to become lighter, healthier, and more energetic. So, he chose the vision that would lead him where he wanted to go: to be fast.

To say we want the image of God restored in us requires us to have a vision for what the image of God looks like. God has many attributes. God is all-powerful and all-knowing. If it were entirely up to us, it would be tempting to choose power as our image of God. We could spend our lives trying to accumulate as much power as possible, and every time we gained power over another person we could reassure ourselves that it was right for us to assert our power because it made us like God. Never mind that people who seek unchecked power are infinitely more likely to become tyrants than saints.

Or, we could choose knowledge as the defining image of God. This path would lead us on a quest to learn as much as we could about everything (which isn't altogether a bad thing) and feeling smugly superior to those poor pitiful folks whose education falls below our arrogant standards (which is a terrible thing). Of course, we all know plenty of people who have plenty of knowledge without much wisdom. They know everything there is to know about facts, figures, and theories, but no one wants to talk to them at a party because all they want to do is to hear themselves talk.

Thankfully, the moral influence theory reminds Christians we have been given a direct vision of the image of God: Jesus Christ - who shows us the defining characteristic of God is love, sacrificial love.

John Wesley, the founder of the Methodist movement in the late 1700s and one of the greatest evangelists and humanitarians the world has ever known, derived from Jesus' life three manifestations of God's image.[33]

The first manifestation was the **natural image** of God. It is God's nature to pursue a relationship with humanity. This is why God became incarnate in the person of Jesus of Nazareth – to pursue us. Within each of us, God has placed the capacity and desire to pursue a conscious relationship with our creator. This is why every culture on earth develops religions and contemplates eternity. Though sin often causes us to pursue a false vision for God, our very pursuit of God is evidence of God's image within us.

The second manifestation Wesley identified was the **political image** of God. God created the world and ordered its functions. Day and night, predator and prey, summer and winter are all part of God's design. Similarly, God endowed humanity with gifts of leadership and management and granted humanity dominion

---

[33] John Wesley, A New Nature in Albert C. Outler and Richard P. Heitzenrater (eds), *John Wesley's Sermons: An Anthology* (Abingdon, 1991), pp. 335-345.

over the earth[34] – the responsibility to use these gifts to create flourishing societies, thriving families, and healthy ecosystems. When we engage in the political process of ordering society with a focus on justice, prosperity, and environmental sustainability, we are living out the political image of God in which we were created.

Lastly, Wesley identified the **moral image** of God. The moral image of God is not a role to fulfill, but a relational orientation which directs us in all our tasks. Through Jesus Christ, we learn the essence of the image of God is love. Yes, God is all-powerful and all-knowing, but God applies all that power and knowledge to the purpose of spreading love and grace throughout the world. As we seek to share with others the same affection God shares with us, we show the world the moral image of God.

New Habits

With a new identity as children of God and a new vision of what it means to be created in the image of God, we now need new habits to constantly push us towards the vision of God's image we have seen in the person of Jesus Christ.

In this endeavor, the moral example theory becomes our guide – reminding us it is not enough to believe in

---

[34] Genesis 1:26

Jesus, we must also live like him if we ever hope to love like he loves.

Diet and exercise became the new habits that gave my friend his energy back. Looking at the life of Christ, we would be foolish to believe we could ever exhibit his sacrificial love without embracing the habits which sustained him.

Jesus dedicated time specifically to prayer and scripture reading each day and sometimes for days at a time. He worshiped in the synagogues each week. He spent hours upon hours with his closest disciples. He gave his tithes to the temple. He sought out the poor, the marginalized, the oppressed, and the foreigners with foreign religions living nearby, and he blessed them.

If you want to see people more and more as God sees them, there's nothing I can tell you to do that will help you more than reading scripture and praying every day. It will change the way you see others. It will change the way you see God. It will even change the way you see you.

If you feel used up and burnt out, there's nowhere I can direct to find as much of the power and inspiration you need to keep going than weekly worship. There's a good reason God created the world in six days and rested on the seventh. There's a good reason why Jesus spent every Sabbath day worshiping in the synagogues regardless of whether he was the one doing the preaching or not. If God created the world like that and Jesus needed to worship at least once a week, you probably do, too.

During the years of his public ministry, Jesus always seemed to be on the go, traveling from town to town. The only constant was the closeness of his disciples and the time they spent together walking the roads, navigating the Sea of Galilee, breaking bread together after a long day of teaching and healing. The disciples were Jesus' small group. On the night before he was arrested, his greatest desire was to share a meal with them.

When he needed to pray for strength to face the ordeal ahead of him, he took some of his disciples with him to the Garden of Gethsemane. If you want to remain grounded and strong, you'll need to find what Jesus had: a small group who will love you, pray for you, and challenge you. Your group doesn't need to look at you as the leader. They just need to love the way they see Jesus working in you.

Jesus was a middle-class carpenter who paid his tithes to the Temple and relied on the generosity of others to support his public ministry. There were countless people in Galilee and Jerusalem with more money than him, but none with more power. If you want his power to be made evident in your life, you'll need to embrace generosity by tithing to your church to support God's work in the world and giving to the organizations who are lifting up the poor and oppressed in your community. Your heart can't remain focused on loving if your wallet is focused mostly on consuming.

Jesus intentionally sought out people who others didn't think were worth his time. He invited himself to the house of the hated tax collector, Zacchaeus. He made an intentional habit of crossing the Sea of Galilee to minister to the Gentiles living on the other side.

He healed entire leper colonies and showed respect to women society looked down upon. If you want to love all people the way Jesus loves them, you'll need to find a way to be around people who don't look like you, don't make the same amount of money as you, don't believe like you, and don't vote like you. Jesus didn't love people in abstraction. He loved people in person.

A New You

With Christ guiding you to embrace a new identity, a new vision, and new habits, you will gradually become a new you – a more Christ-like you – a you who is at one with your gifts, your shortcomings, your calling, and your God.

Before you dive into the next chapter, take a moment to ask yourself:

- What identity do I live out of? Does it need to change?
- What's my vision for my life? Is it a worthy vision? Does it come out of God's vision for me?
- What are my most deep-seated habits? Are they taking me where I want to go? Are they helping me become more like Christ?

When you can answer these questions, you'll be ready to find your place at the table in God's family which is the topic of Chapter 5, *The Family You Never Knew You Had*.

CHAPTER FIVE
The Family You Never Knew You Had

Before I was married, older folks always made a habit of reminding me, "Now, remember, you date a person, but you marry a family."

At the time, I had no idea how right they were. Today, after almost two decades of marriage, their wisdom seems so obvious.

Thankfully, the perfect person and the perfect family all came in the same package for me.

My wife's family is awesome. I came from a small family. They've got more cousins, second cousins, aunts, and uncles than you can count. My family is spread out. Most of her family lives near one another. My family members live in small houses in cities. Her family lives in big houses on the family farm.

Whenever we go visit, there's always something to do: some improvement that needs to be completed, some cousin playing in a ball game, some adventure awaiting.

On the rare occasion when all the projects are complete, there's plenty of people to visit. No sooner do our wheels hit the gravel driveway than family members begin to descend upon my in-law's house to visit.

In a big family like that it's hard to feel sorry for yourself because you're never the only one going through tough times. And it's hard to get too big for your britches because there's always someone else accomplishing something amazing, especially the young ones who seemingly fly through milestones and rites of passage in the blink of an eye.

I never could have imagined a better family to marry into. From the moment my wife stood at the altar and chose me to be her husband, they have accepted me as if I had always been one of their own.

Adopted into Jesus' Family

As Jesus hung on the cross, he looked down to see John, his disciple, standing next to his mother, Mary. Gathering up his strength to speak, he addressed his mother saying, "Woman, here is your son."[35] Then turning to his disciple he said, "Here is your mother."[36]

On the surface, these might appear be the most practical words of Jesus recorded from the cross. He

---

[35] John 19:26

[36] John 19:27

knew he would not be around to provide financial and emotional support to his mom. So, he designated his most trustworthy disciple to look after her.

On the other hand, we also know from the Bible that Jesus had other brothers who could have taken care of their mom, so it's quite possible Jesus was speaking primarily on a much deeper level. Perhaps Jesus was telling John, his mom, and all of us who would one day seek to be disciples that following him means becoming part of a new family.

Such a message would certainly be consistent with his earlier statement that "Whoever does the will of my Father in heaven is my brother and sister and mother."[37]

I believe when Jesus gave his life on the cross, he was choosing each of us to become a part of his family just as my wife stood at the altar and chose me to become a part of her family. When we stand at the church altar and publicly profess our faith in Jesus as our Lord and Savior, we are choosing to accept the invitation to become a part of Jesus' family that he made to us long ago on the cross. Once we do so, we become just as much a part of Jesus' family as anyone.

The way in which Jesus' death incorporates us into the family of God is an aspect of atonement which has received regrettably little attention over the years from

---

[37] Matthew 12:50

Christian theologians. While theories of atonement regarding how Jesus' death defeats evil, forgives sins, and offers personal salvation abound, few theories of atonement focus on how Jesus' death invites us to become a part of a family and what communal life should look like within our new family. I like to think of the way Jesus' death invites us into the family of God as **the adoption theory of atonement.**[38]

While humanity's first sin (when Adam and Eve ate the forbidden fruit in the garden of Eden) severed their intimacy with God, humanity's second sin (when Cain murdered his brother Abel) introduced division into the human family system God designed for us to live in. All the -isms which divide and destroy families and nations – egotism, racism, sexism, nationalism, imperialism, even denominationalism – stem from the dysfunction wrought upon the human family by Cain's crime.

For Jesus to truly atone for the sins of humanity, his death must have the power to reconcile humanity with one another as well as with God. On the cross, Jesus dies for the victims of injustice (the Abel's of the world) and for their oppressors (the Cain's of the world). From the top of Golgotha, he issues each person an undeserved

---

[38] To my knowledge, I am coining the phrase: the adoption theory of atonement. While adoption is a key theme in Christian theology, it is generally considered within other theories of atonement from an individualistic perspective focusing personal salvation rather than a communal perspective centered around the new relational norms established for Christ followers. If others have previously used the phrase the adoption theory of atonement in reference to a particular aspect of Jesus' saving work on the cross, their writings have escaped the scope of my research.

invitation into the family of God. By drawing oppressor and oppressed into one family, Jesus overcomes the divisions within the human family brought about by "eye for an eye," "tooth for a tooth," zero-sum thinking.

In Jesus' sacrifice, the oppressed discover the respect and self-worth of someone for whom the Son of God willingly gave his life, and the oppressors find forgiveness for which they could have never asked. When gazing upon the perfect life of Christ and his selfless death, each person comes to see himself as both oppressor and oppressed, and in Christ they learn to offer the healing and forgiveness they have found in him to others.

This is not to imply that each person is equally oppressor and oppressed. It is rather to note that in recognizing our own capacity to oppress, even if on a smaller scale, we find the humility to look upon those who oppress on a larger scale and say, "There but by the grace of God go I." And it is precisely this humility which opens the door for eventual reconciliation.

One of Jesus' most famous stories is of two brothers. The younger brother treats the family with unfathomable disrespect, squanders much of the family fortune, and ends up destitute in a foreign land. Meanwhile, the ultra-responsible older brother does everything he is supposed to do. Years later, when the now penitent younger brother returns home, the father joyously welcomes him back as the incredulous older brother looks on. The story ends without revealing whether the older brother ever accepted his younger sibling fully back into the family, but it leaves no doubt God the Father desired for him to do so.[39]

If God's way of putting the human family back together through the death of His Son seems highly unorthodox and even a little unfair to you, it's because it is. It also might be the only way that could ever work.

Just What Kind of Family Is This?

Every family has a matriarch or patriarch. Usually, they are from the oldest living generation of the family, though not always. To identify the matriarch or patriarch of a family, you simply need to find the person who plays the most influential role in setting the values, traditions, and unwritten rules by which the family abides. They are the glue that holds the family together.

You might not find it worth the money to fly back into town every Thanksgiving just to see your cousins, but you'll do it gladly to make sure you don't disappoint Grandma. And when you become infuriated with another family member, there is very little in this world that can motivate you to forgive as much as the pained expression on Grandpa's face every time

---

[39] Luke 15:11-32

he thinks about the conflict. When the matriarch and patriarch die, often family gatherings split up into smaller units with their own matriarchs and patriarchs from younger generations.

For the Christian family, Jesus is the patriarch who sets the values, traditions, and rules for the family. Ever since his death, his followers have been charged with sharing his family values with their families and communities. Among the most prominent characteristics the Christian family derives from Jesus' life are equality, intimacy, and royalty.

Equality

If you have attended church more than once or twice in your life, you've probably heard a preacher say, "The ground at the foot of the cross is flat." While blatantly untrue from a historical perspective, Jesus was by all accounts crucified on a hill outside Jerusalem, there are few statements as true as this one theologically.

On these occasions the preacher isn't talking about the geography of the crucifixion site, but rather the fact that we all approach the cross in equal need of grace. It's hard to feel superior to anyone when you recognize your sins were such that the Son of God had to die in order for you to be forgiven.

The egalitarian nature of Jesus' movement made it

counter-cultural in his day, and perhaps just as much so today. In a highly patriarchal culture, Jesus was the first Jewish rabbi to allow female disciples to follow him. While teaching among the Jewish scribes and pharisees, Jesus lifted up a hated Samaritan as the example of faithfully loving your neighbor as yourself.[40] And after hearing the pleas of a Roman army officer seeking healing for his servant, Jesus says he has never seen such faith in all of Israel.[41]

It's understandable that Jesus' followers might struggle to embody equality while living in a world of extreme inequalities. Nonetheless, it's sad that many times, even those who claim to be members of Jesus' family created through the cross, take offense at Jesus' most egalitarian teachings.

First among Jesus' most offensive teachings is a story known as The Workers in the Vineyard.[42] In this story, Jesus speaks of a vineyard owner who hires workers in the morning to work a full day for a full day's wage. About midday, he hires more workers to help in the vineyard and again in the late afternoon, he brings in even more workers to finish the day's tasks. With the work done, the owners instruct the laborers to line up to be paid, beginning with the ones who arrived latest.

---

[40] Luke 10:25-37

[41] Matthew 8:5-13

[42] Matthew 20:1-16

When the those who only worked a few hours receive a full day's wage, expectations rise from the those in the back of the line who worked all day and naturally begin calculating how much they will receive. Then to everyone's surprise, the owner pays those who worked a half day and a full day the exact same as those who worked only in the evening. Every worker receives one full day's wage.

As you might imagine, those who worked a full day become enraged. How come the other workers got paid just as much for less work?

The story ends with the owner dismissing their selfish concerns by reminding them they were paid everything they were owed and chastising them for their jealously towards those who did not have the opportunity to work for the entire day.

The implications are clear: In the Kingdom of God, those with impeccable moral resumes – who find faith early in life and those with a checkered past who find it later – receive the same reward.

Does this story anger you? Do you find yourself saying, "But that's not fair!"

If so, you're not the first. Nor will you be the last.

We often are guilty of overlaying the inequalities of our world onto our conceptions of the Kingdom of God.

I grew up hearing a lot about mansions in glory. The idea many people held was that super-Christians like Mother Teresa would inherit large mansions in heaven, while regular Christians would receive modest homes in a great zip code. Of course, if you know much about Mother Teresa, you know that she would be quite displeased if she were to receive better accommodations than her neighbors. In my mind's eye, I can see her fussing at the angels for building her such a large edifice while neglecting to do the same for others. Then I imagine her walking up and down the streets of gold inviting those with smaller homes to come live with her in her mansion.

While, in all seriousness, I always figured the idea of mansions in glory was figurative language, I have often found myself subconsciously believing that there were super-spiritual people who would forevermore enjoy greater intimacy with God and a higher place in God's family than the rest of us.

At least, this is how I thought until I became a dad. Currently, I have three school-age children living in my house. They each have different gifts and they each have their own unique ways of inspiring, amazing, and occasionally infuriating me. They are all over the map when it comes to their natural inclination to obey family rules, academic performance in school, and athletic prowess. If I didn't know better, I'd wonder how they could be from the same family.

Yet, their differences and even their mistakes do not cause me to love them any more or any less. From the moment they were born I loved them as much as a parent could possibly love a child, simply because they were mine. Nor do they receive a better room in my house or a bigger college fund at the bank because of their behavior. What kind of awful parent would value one child more than another? Not you. Not me. And not God the Father.

For his part, Jesus only talks about one mansion in glory: his Father's house in which there are many rooms, enough space for all of us.[43] In so doing, he gives us a healthier and more accurate image of heaven. We do not serve God to acquire a higher place in the eternal pecking order. We serve God because doing so is its own reward.

Intimacy

If we are going to be living down the hall from each other for eternity, it will help tremendously if we learn to enjoy and respect one another.

The inequalities of our world have a way of pushing us into small enclaves of like-minded, like-colored,

---

[43] John 14:2

like-resourced people with whom we feel safe enough to be real. We perceive most everyone else to be too much of a threat to let our guard down around. As a result, many of us live relationally impoverished lives while a wealth of opportunities for friendship and companionship pass us by.

Jesus had a way of intimately including outsiders. From his deep theological conversation with the Samaritan woman at the well to his invitation to Matthew, the tax collector, to become a disciple, he found a way to form intimate connections across the boundaries imposed by society. In his death, he provides us all with a common connection great enough to overcome any externally or internally imposed barrier.

When I was in seminary, I served for one semester as a hospital chaplain. Part of the job required me to meet each week with my supervisor and a group of other novice chaplains for training and reflection. As part of our group time, we would often present case studies to give our fellow chaplains a chance to affirm our work and/or challenge us to do better.

One day, one of my fellow chaplains, who happened to be a middle-aged black lady, presented a case study of her work with a patient to us. When she was done, the supervisor, who himself was a middle-aged black man, asked us all to give her feedback. I told her I thought she had done very well. The supervisor subsequently dismissed our class, but as I packed up my things I heard him say, "Wil, please hang around for a moment. I need to talk to you."

No sooner had everyone else left the room than he lit into me: "Why didn't you challenge her about her case study? I know you thought she made some significant mistakes. I saw it on your face as she was talking. But you said nothing. Why?"

"Look," I replied. "I'm a young white male and she's a middle-aged black woman. If I challenge her, I'm going to be seen as a racist and sexist bigot who doesn't respect his elders."

"I figured as much," he said. "Now, you listen here. I know you well enough to know you never would have allowed a white guy your age to get away with that, and you shouldn't have allowed her to do so. By not challenging her, you weren't respecting her. You weren't helping her. You were patronizing her and preventing her from having the chance to learn how to be a great chaplain. I'm going to have her go back over her case study next time we are together and if you don't challenge her then, I'll cut your grade."

Needless to say, I did some soul searching that weekend. I had to find a way to muster the courage to push back against some barriers which scared me to death. I found the strength I needed in the narratives of Jesus' crucifixion.

As I walked into the hospital for the meeting I had been dreading, I reminded myself, "Jesus didn't die on the cross so I could have superficial relationships with older black women. Jesus died to break down every barrier which separates us from intimately connecting with one another."

Full Disclosure: My colleague did not seem especially happy when I challenged her to think about her interaction with patients from a different perspective. For a couple weeks after that encounter, there was an undeniable tension in our relationship.

By the end of the semester, however, we had both learned how to challenge each other to think differently while also finding a way to relate to one another which was more open, honest, and empathetic than we ever could have achieved through polite indifference.

Are there people in your life you treat with polite indifference or unacknowledged bias? Is it time for you to find strength through the cross of Christ to relate in a different way? A better way? The Jesus way?

Royalty

One of the saddest things you'll ever witness is when someone accepts Christ into their life and then becomes more bigoted because of it. They experience forgiveness and the assurance of salvation, but fail to incorporate Jesus' teachings on community into their lives.

It's not hard to see how this can happen. I've been in many churches where it appears the folks in attendance believe Jesus came to save the church and to send the rest of the world straight to hell. Since everyone else is most likely condemned – and quite misguided – it's only natural for them to feel superior to those pitiful souls who haven't yet seen the light.

Such an orientation towards the world demonstrates a misunderstanding of Jesus' teachings about church and kingdom.

The Gospels only record Jesus mentioning the word church twice. Once in Matthew 16:18 when he tells Peter he will build the church on the confession that he is the Son of God, and once again in Matthew 18:17 while discussing how to handle a church member who persists in unrepentant sinful living.

On the other hand, Jesus speaks of God's kingdom over 100 times in the Gospels. This means if you were alive in Jesus' day and had the opportunity to hear him speak, it is almost certain you would have heard him talk about the kingdom, but doubtful you ever would have heard him mention the church.

Many Christians assume the Kingdom of God and the

church are one in the same thing. But in Jesus' account, the two are quite different. In fact, it's crucial we recognize the difference between the kingdom and the church if we are to understand the royal nature of the family Jesus has invited us to join.

For Jesus, the Kingdom of God, which in Matthew's Gospel he refers to as the Kingdom of heaven, is all encompassing. He often says the Kingdom of God has come near as if you can't escape it even you want to. He also begins many of his teachings by saying, "The Kingdom of God/heaven is like...."

Everyone lives in God's Kingdom. Like earthly kingdoms, not everyone is happy about it and not everyone is a citizen. But everyone lives within it.

Similarly, the kingdom of God has certain standards and ways of operating. Those who choose other standards do so at considerable risk.

The church, on the other hand, is comprised of the people who have specifically pledged themselves to live by the kingdom's standards. These people have gained citizenship in the kingdom and have become part of "a chosen race, a royal priesthood, a holy nation, God's own people."[44]

Drawing on the language of 1st Peter, we might say

---

[44] 1 Peter 2:9

those within the church are members of a royal family. Like all royal families, their job is not simply to seek their own security and prosperity, but to work for the good of the kingdom.

Churches which focus more on condemning the world than blessing the world would do well to remember the Bible verse which comes immediately after the most famous verse: "Indeed, God did not send the Son into the world to condemn the world, but in order that the world might be saved through him."[45]

I am not arguing here that Jesus' work on the cross should lead us to adopt the universalist belief that all people will be granted eternal salvation. Though attractive for a number of reasons, I am not sure how to square universalism with a fair reading of the Gospels. In many of Jesus' teachings, it appears he clearly indicates God will not force grace upon those who appear hellbent to reject it.

I am convinced, however, that what we see of Jesus in the Gospels teaches us that the saving and sanctifying work of God is active and ongoing in the lives of many who will most likely never join a Christian church.

In other words, Jesus offers his followers the assurance of salvation. He does not give us the assurance of everyone else's damnation.

---

[45] John 3:17

If it bothers you not to have an easy formula to know exactly who is saved, I'm sorry to break it to you, but only God knows that. What we can be assured of, like the workers in the vineyard, is that we are guaranteed God will give us what God has promised and if God wants to give more to others than we would have imagined, our only response should be to rejoice.

Royal Family Dysfunction

If the church is a royal family, what happens when the royals lose their way and go off the rails?

No sooner was the church established than it began to be corrupted. Many of Paul's New Testament letters deal with corruption and immorality in the fledgling Christian churches.

Like any organization, we could get all the corruption out of the church if we just got all the people out of the church. Of course, then we wouldn't have a church at all.

So, what is God's response to a corrupt church?

God has amazing patience with the church, but God will not protect the church from the consequences of its failures.

While we can trace many of the great strides for civil rights and free society to the influence of Christianity, we also live in a world where many churches have used the Bible to justify racism and slavery, where Christian slave owners were considered to be more cruel than their secular counterparts, and where still today white Christians are more likely than white non-Christians to believe in white supremacy.[46] On top of all that, we now know for centuries the church used its power and privilege to enable and cover up child sexual abuse.

Good grief! Perhaps the best assurance God won't give up on the church in the future is that God hasn't given up yet, even though we have provided no shortage of motivation for doing so.

When a royal family goes bad, changes must occur or the kingdom will eventually crumble.

In my country, many church leaders, including me, bemoan the declining influence of the church and the decreasing percentage of the population who identify as practicing Christians. I spend every day thinking about, praying about, and working to help more people come to faith in Jesus Christ and become involved in a local church. Yet, based on historical precedent, I can't help but wonder if God might not see things differently on a societal level.

In the Old Testament, God was willing to allow Jerusalem to be ransacked and the Jewish people to be led away to exile in Babylon so that a faithful remnant

---

[46] Robert P. Jones, *White Too Long: The Legacy of White Supremacy in American Christianity* (Simon & Schuster, 2020), pp. 84-88, 155-187.

could return to rebuild faithfully. I wonder if this might be what is happening currently in White American Christianity.

When the church ceases to work for the good of the kingdom, the church must be reformed. Could it be that God will use the current declines to rebuild the church in our society so that the defining descriptors of its witness will no longer be "white" or "American," but simply "Christian"?

Your Place in the Family

While you may have some differences of opinion with my take on White American Christianity, and while admittedly it's always difficult to clearly discern the work of God in the affairs of nations in the current moment, life is not quite so ambiguous on the local level.

The Bible is quite clear that Jesus has broken down the barriers which separate us from intimate relationships of equality and has adopted those who commit their lives to following the way of Jesus into a royal family.

All of which means we have some very important questions to ask ourselves.

How does it change your understanding of God's calling on your life to know that you've been invited into a royal family with all the rights and responsibilities that go along with it? Who is God calling you to befriend? Who is God calling you to bless? How is God calling your church to bless the world rather than condemn it?

CHAPTER SIX

For All

The morning of April 6, 2015, I jumped into a car with two of my good friends. We headed north out of Knoxville, Tennessee towards Kentucky en route to our final destination of Indianapolis, Indiana. That evening in Indianapolis our alma mater Duke University was playing the University of Wisconsin in the finals of the men's college basketball tournament for the right to become national champions. And we were planning to be at the game to cheer them on.

We had plenty of gas in the tank, snacks for the road, a hotel room lined up for the evening, and we left in plenty of time to arrive hours before tip-off. Only one small problem remained. We had no tickets, and no one gets into the game without tickets.

Our lack of tickets hardly dampened our enthusiasm. We had each saved up a little extra spending money and we were sure with hours to walk to the streets around the stadium we would be able to find someone, most likely a fan from one of the teams which lost in the semifinals, who would be willing to sell us tickets for decent seats at a decent price.

We were sadly mistaken.

Shortly after arriving at the stadium, we realized the entire state of Wisconsin had descended upon Indianapolis and bought up all the tickets for this momentous occasion. The tickets that were available, were more than we could afford and so far away from the court they would require binoculars to decipher the action. We each had a generous, but firm, limit our wives would allow us to spend on tickets. As many of the ticket prices far exceeded our monthly mortgage bills and with our spending limits far below our house payments, our options looked bleak.

After hours of looking for a deal, we began to resign ourselves to the fact we had just driven five hours to watch the game on television from a restaurant. Until, as luck would have it, we overheard some Wisconsin fans talking about how the stadium ticket office had just released a new batch of recently returned tickets at face value for excellent seats.

We knew this was our chance. We had to get to the ticket office which was over half a mile from our current location as quickly as possible. Being a competitive runner, my presence came in handy at this moment for my non-runner friends. I sprinted around the stadium to secure our place in the ticket line while also gaining the assurance my friends would never again pick on me for my dedication to a hobby most people consider punishment.

Note to reader: I promise I will eventually relate this story to atonement. For now, just stick with me. It's a really good story.

As we inched closer in line, we could see the people ahead of us celebrating as they purchased their tickets. Finally, it was our turn. We approached the ticket office window with relief on our faces. We'd made it. Our journey was a success. We were going to be able to watch the game together.

"Three tickets together, please." We told the attendant.

"Sorry, boys, we're fresh out. I sold the last tickets to the group ahead of you." He replied.

"Will you be releasing any more tickets?" we asked.

"Not sure," he said. "Maybe. No guarantees."

Dejected, we walked away. Our last best chance to get into the game was gone.

We began to evaluate our strategy. Should we call it quits now and go looking for a good seat near the TV at a sports bar? Should we walk the streets a little more hoping a seller would get desperate with tip-off approaching?

Then one of my friends had an idea. "I think we should stand right here and smile politely at the box office guy. He's got to feel bad for us. I'll bet he'll try to help us if he can." For lack of a better idea, we agreed.

Turns out, my friend was right. Several minutes later, the box office attendant motioned for us. Three tickets on the lower level had become available for a price well below what we had planned to spend. We were thrilled. Our wives were thrilled (with the price). He was thrilled to see three grown men jumping up and down like little boys.

Soon thereafter, we entered the stadium and presented our tickets to the ushers. We were in row XX. Probably the top row of the lower level, we figured. But the usher didn't take us up. He took us down. Down past the rows of people who paid 10 times as much for their tickets as we did. Down further past the parents of the players. Down past the credentialed media. Down to the row right above our team's bench!

Upon arriving at our row, the usher promptly set out folding chairs for us. Turns out the stadium usually kept the area where we were sitting open just in case it was needed for extra media or handicapped seating for family and dignitaries. The box office guy had literally created seats which weren't previously available for us!

How our fortunes had changed! Suddenly, other people with great seats were offering us four digits sums just to switch spots. We high-fived the players as they came out for warm-ups. Celebrities walked past us to get to their seats at center court. I had a nice conversation with former Republican Presidential nominee Mitt Romney as I stood to allow him to walk past me to his seat.

"Hi, Mitt. It's good to see you. Glad you could make it the game tonight," I said while reaching out to shake his hand.

"Nice to see you too," he responded and then continued to his seat.

(I'm pretty sure I made a big impression. If the game wasn't just about to start, he probably would have wanted to hang around longer to talk with me.)

As the game began, we texted our friends to inform them we were on the front row. None of them believed us. They thought our texts were just a well-coordinated prank until the television cameras panned the area behind the team benches and there we were staring right back at them.

By the end of the evening, confetti rained down the rafters. Our team won the game. We had a memory to last a lifetime. And it all happened because a box office attendant took pity on three friends who really wanted to see the game and created space for us.

Creating Space

During the Protestant Reformation, as newly formed denominations began establishing their official doctrine, debates raged about just how much space Jesus' death had created for persons to enter the Kingdom of God.

Followers of John Calvin, most of whose denominations later became known as Reformed or Presbyterian, began to promote an idea which came to be known as *limited atonement*. In their thinking, God was all powerful and therefore, God could accomplish anything God desired. If God wanted to save someone from their sins, God would assuredly do so. Accordingly, Jesus' grace was irresistible because how could humans possibly resist the grace an all-powerful God desired for them to received?

This way of thinking created a conundrum regarding how to understand the substantial percentage of the world population who refused to acknowledge the divinity of Christ and follow his ways. If grace was irresistible, why did so many people seemingly resist it?

Calvinists solved this logical problem with limited atonement – the idea that Jesus did not die to atone for the sins of the whole world. Jesus died solely to atone for the sins of the elect, those who were predestined to accept his grace and lordship for themselves.

Some Calvinists even took these beliefs so far as to argue God enjoyed inflicting damnation upon those who were not elected to eternal life, and that those who were not predestined to eternal salvation should be thankful for their few years to enjoy worldly pleasure on earth before spending eternity in misery. A few Calvinist leaders pushed back against these extreme views of predestination by arguing Jesus' death was powerful enough to atone for all, but was meant only for those God already knew would be willing to receive it.

In support of limited atonement, Calvinists cite scriptures like John 17 where Jesus prays, "I am not asking on behalf of the world, but on behalf of those you gave me, because they are yours.... While I was with them, I protected them in your name that You have given me. I guarded them, and not one of them was lost except the one destined to be lost."[47]

While belief in limited atonement and predestination provided an intellectually satisfying answer for Calvinists, it left a bad taste in the mouth of most other Christian traditions.

Starting with the works of Jacob Arminius in the 1600s and continuing through the teachings of John

---

[47] John 17:9,12.

Wesley and the hymns of his brother Charles Wesley in the 1700s, Protestant voices rose up to offer an alternative view: unlimited atonement.

According to proponents of unlimited atonement, God is all powerful and Jesus' death is sufficient to atone for the sins of all humanity. Humanity, however, has enough free will to resist God's grace. Thankfully, humanity also lives under God's prevenient grace (the grace given to all prior to conversion) which provides humanity with the power to accept the gift of God's saving grace given through the cross of Jesus Christ.

Advocates of unlimited atonement support their position by referring to Biblical passages such as 1 John 2:1-2:

> *But if anyone does sin, we have an advocate with the Father, Jesus Christ the righteous; and he is the atoning sacrifice for our sins, and not for ours only but also for the sins of the whole world.*

The debate between limited and unlimited atonement is a debate in which the very nature of God is at stake. Is God like that gracious, wonderful ticket booth attendant in Indianapolis who created extra space in the stadium for three guys who could not afford entrance otherwise? Or did God create a set number of spaces in the Kingdom reserved only for the fortunate elect?

If you're like me, it's hard to imagine God as revealed

through Jesus not being at least as gracious as a ticket booth worker.

Can you imagine bringing children into this world if beforehand you knew they would be condemned to eternal damnation? I cannot.

When we began our family, my wife and I knew our children would grow one day to have minds of their own. We knew they might well make choices which would break our hearts and even God's heart. And we acknowledged the possibility they might choose to turn away from God for all eternity. But we chose to become parents in the strong hope we would raise children who would learn to love God and their families.

If we had known, however, that our children would be predestined for damnation no matter what, you can bet we would have done everything in our power to ensure we never had kids. Out of compassion, we would have forgone the joys of parenthood to save our kids from eternal suffering without a second thought. To say that God brings people into the world who are predestined for damnation is to say that God is not even as compassionate as imperfect people like us.

Furthermore, it's interesting to me that while I have met many people who claim to be predestined for heaven, I've never met anyone who claims to be predestined for damnation.

What Difference Does It Really Make?

I imagine some of you may be wondering if this debate between limited and unlimited atonement has any real merit. Whatever we believe about God doesn't change God. If God wants to save people, God can save people whether we believe God should or not.

Yes, God can save people with or without our approval. Thank God!

What we believe about God, however, does change us and how we treat one another.

Believing you are part of the elect predestined for salvation while others are predestined for damnation is a small step from believing those others constitute a lower class of humanity deserving of less rights and privileges.

As I mentioned in the previous chapter, one of the most disturbing aspects of American Christianity is that before the abolition of slavery, Christian slave owners were known to be more violent towards their slaves than non-Christian slave masters. There are even numerous accounts of slave owners who converted to Christianity and, rather than immediately setting their slaves free, subsequently became significantly more cruel towards them.

Why? The Christian slave owners believed they had a

divine right to abuse their slaves, while the non-Christian slave owners only believed they had a legal right to be cruel. When you think you are divinely ordained to a higher level of humanity than someone else, it's easy to grow numb to even the most basic moral impulses.

Remember Who You Are Talking To

Whenever Christians interact with anyone, we should do so within the acknowledgment we are dealing with someone of sacred worth for whom Jesus Christ gave his life.

This is why I consider myself anti-abortion, anti-poverty, anti-racist, anti-death penalty, anti-war, anti-unrealistically high health care costs, anti-discrimination, and anti-anything that strips away dignity from human life. Those are lives for whom Christ died. Who are we to treat others as if they deserve less than the respect and consideration due a child of God?

It's also why I pray every day that God will lead me in my personal interactions to treat others with empathy and respect. While I fail often, I pray each day the way I love my neighbors might become a little closer to the way Jesus loves us all.

I recognize you might not agree with every way I seek to live out my Christian faith. You no doubt have your own list of anti's and some of my anti's may not appear on your list; not because you love Jesus less than me, but because you understand the political realities of our world differently than I do.

If so, that's okay. If we were face to face, I would enjoy the chance to talk through our differing understandings, learn from you, and hopefully offer you something of value from my perspective.

Since we're not able to have a personal conversation right now, however, here's what I would ask. Take an inventory of your political ideology and interpersonal relationships. Then ask yourself:

- Do all the political policies I support align with my belief that every person is an equally valued child of God?
- Do my personal ways of relating to others communicate the respect and dignity Jesus would want me to show for someone for whom he gave his life?

Remember Who You Are

In order to recognize Jesus' love for others, we must also remember Jesus' love for us.

When Jesus prayed in the Garden of Gethsemane for his Father to provide a way other than crucifixion to atone for the sins of the world, his prayer would have been answered if there had been another way. There wasn't a less costly way because of the depth of the sins of the world and the depth of each of our sins.

Jesus had to die for the sins of the world and he had to die for the sins of each one of us.

It's true. "All have sinned and fall short of the glory of God."[48]

All of us needed his death to atone for our sins and make a way for us to be at one with God, with our neighbors, and with ourselves.

Whenever you see a cross, remind yourself it was for the world and it was for me.

So, when you have a chance to make a difference for good in the world and you're tempted to shrink away in fear of failure, remember who died to give you that chance.

When you violate values you hold dear, and shame overwhelms you, remember who gave his life so your sins could be removed from you as far as the east is from the west.

And when you are tempted to feel superior to others with beliefs and habits you don't fully understand, remember Jesus died for you and for all.

---

[48] Romans 3:23

Epilogue

On Easter morning as the disciples were discussing reports of an empty tomb, a very different conversation was taking place in the temple where priests gathered to discuss what to do about the large curtain which had inexplicably torn in two Friday afternoon.

I imagine their conversation vacillated between the practical and theological. Why had the curtain torn from top to bottom? Was it shoddy craftsmanship? Did the small earthquake cause the fastenings to torque the curtain beyond its breaking point? Was it a sign from God? Could it be mended? Did it need to be replaced entirely? How much would it cost? Such a large, thick curtain would have been exceedingly expensive to replicate. Did they have enough money in the temple treasury to pay for a new one? Would they need to organize a special offering?

The primary role of the curtain was to separate the

Holy of Holies, where the Ark of the Covenant had been kept in the first Temple, from the rest of the Temple. Once a year on Yom Kippur, the Day of Atonement, the High Priest would venture behind the curtain to make incense and blood offerings to atone for the sins of the people.

Little did they know a sacrifice had been made on Golgotha to atone for the sins of the world which would render all future temple sacrifices obsolete. The curtain could be replaced, but a new curtain could never serve the same purpose as the old one. The temple's sacrificial system had been replaced by a once-and-for-all sacrifice by the Son of God to put humanity at one with God and one another.

The Gospel of John concludes by acknowledging the impossibility of one single voice being able to provide adequate testimony to the entirety of Jesus' work.

> *There are also many other things that Jesus did; if every one of them were written down, I suppose the world itself could not contain the books that would be written.*[49]

In this book, I have presented many theories of atonement originally formulated to be contradictory to one another as being largely complimentary instead. I have done so out of my belief that, while some theories may be

---
[49] John 21:25

more helpful and theologically accurate than others, each theory of atonement mentioned in these pages provides us with a single perspective on Jesus' death and that no single perspective can give a full accounting of the enormity of Jesus' saving work of atoning for our sins and reconciling us to God through the cross.

It is my hope that as we learn to view the cross of Christ from the multiple vantage points provided to us through the Biblical witness and the reflections faithful disciples from across the millennia who have come before us, that we might gain a fuller understanding of the costly gift we have been given, and find ourselves led to the same conclusion as the Roman Centurion who, while serving as the commanding officer in charge of overseeing the crucifixion, gazed upon Jesus' lifeless body suspended on the cross and concluded: "Truly this man was God's Son!"[50]

---

[50] Mark 15:39

Grow Your Faith

with these books from Market Square

marketsquarebooks.com

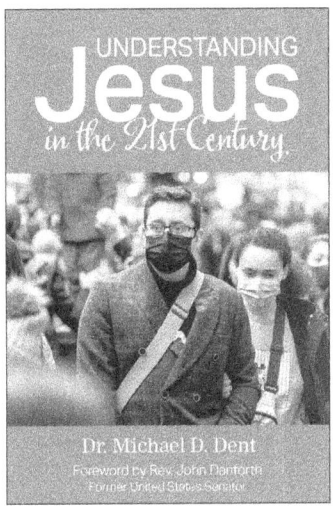

**Understanding Jesus
in the 21st Century**

Michael Dent

Shift 2.0

Phil Maynard

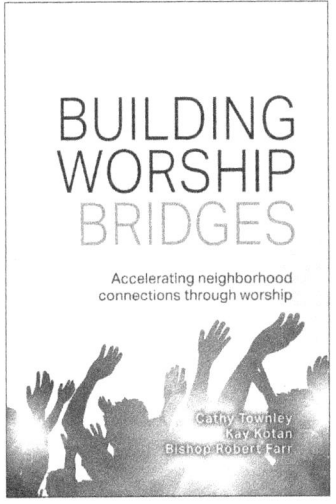

**Building Worship
Bridges**

Cathy Townley

**Get Out of
That Box!**

Anne Bosarge

Grow Your Faith

with these books from Market Square

marketsquarebooks.com

Discipler

Phil Maynard & Eddie Pipkin

Hear It, See It, Risk It

Steve Cordle

A Christian Teenager's Guide to Surviving High School

Ashley Conner

Understanding Your Call

11 Biblical Figures Understand Their Calls from God

by 10 United Methodist Leaders

Other Books
from Market Square
marketsquarebooks.com

Wesleyan Grace Theology

Dr. Donald Haynes

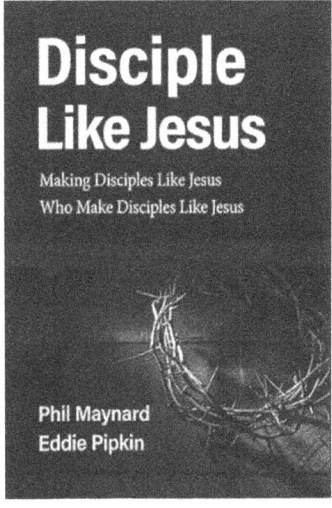

Disciple Like Jesus

Phil Maynard & Eddie Pipkin

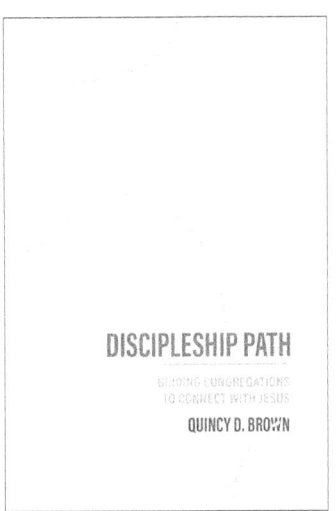

Discipleship Path

Quincy Brown

The Methodist Story Volume I • 1703-1791

Dr. Donald Haynes

More Titles
from Market Square Books
marketsquarebooks.com

Dream Like Jesus
Bring the Impossible to Life

Rebekah Simon-Peter

From Franchise
To Local Dive

Jason Moore & Rosario Picardo

The Methodist Story
Volume 2 • 1792-2019

Dr. Donald W. Haynes

Mission Possible

Kay Kotan and Blake Bradford

Celebrate Christian Seasons

with these books from Market Square

marketsquarebooks.com

Journey to Transformation
2021 Lenten Journey

Bishop Sharma D. Lewis

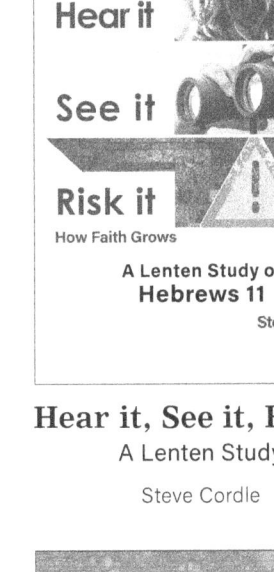

Hear it, See it, Risk it
A Lenten Study

Steve Cordle

HOPE
An Advent Journey

Olu Brown

Tidings of Comfort and Joy
New Stories of Advent & Christmas

Charles W. Maynard

Other Books by Wil Cantrell

Author of ATONE

marketsquarebooks.com

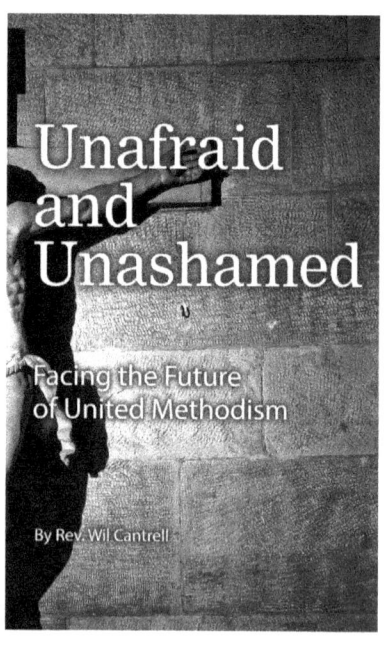

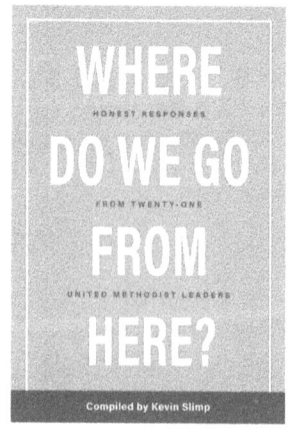

www.ingramcontent.com/pod-product-compliance
Lightning Source LLC
Chambersburg PA
CBHW070814100426
42742CB00012B/2361